Border Wars and Foreign Excursions

The
MILITARY HISTORY
of the
UNITED STATES

Christopher Chant

Border Wars and
Foreign Excursions

MARSHALL CAVENDISH
NEW YORK · LONDON · TORONTO · SYDNEY

Library Edition Published 1992

© Marshall Cavendish Limited 1992

Published by
Marshall Cavendish Corporation
2415 Jerusalem Avenue
PO Box 587
North Bellmore
New York 11710

Series created by Graham Beehag Book Design

Series Editor	Maggi McCormick
Consultant Editors	James R. Arnold
	Roberta Wiener
Sub Editor	Julie Cairns
Designer	Graham Beehag
Illustrators	John Batchelor
	Steve Lucas
	Terry Forest
	Colette Brownrigg
Indexer	Mark Dartford

The publishers wish to thank the following organizations
who have supplied photographs:

The National Archives, Washington. United States
Navy, United States Marines, United States Army,
United States Air Force, Department of Defense,
Library of Congress, The Smithsonian Institution.

The publishers gratefully thank the U.S. Army Military
History Institute, Carlisle Barracks, PA. for the use of
archive material for the following witness accounts:

Page 26-27
*Reminiscences and Thrilling Stories of the War by
Returned Heroes* by James Rankin Young, (Chicago,
1899).

Page 44-45
*Reminiscences and Thrilling Stories of the War by
Returned Heroes* by James Rankin Young, (Chicago,
1899).

Library of Congress Cataloging-in-Publication Data

Chant, Christopher.
    The Military History of the United States / Christopher Chant –
Library ed.
        p. cm.
    Includes bibliographical references and index.
    Summary: Surveys the wars that have directly influenced the
United States., from the Revolutionary War through the Cold War.
    ISBN 1-85435-358-6 ISBN 1-85435-361-9 (set)
    1. United States - History, Military - Juvenile literature.
[1. United States - History, Military.] I. Title.
t181.C52 1991
973 - dc20   90 - 19547
                                                        CIP
                                                        AC

Printed in Singapore by Times Offset PTE Ltd
Bound in the United States

Contents

U ntil the last quarter of the 19th century, the United States of America had been largely inward-looking, both emotionally and politically. From about 1875, however, the country began to evolve from a continental power into a world power in a shift led by the development of trade between the U.S. and other countries. By the late 1880s, an increasingly large number of Americans had begun to realize that the time had come to break with the country's traditional isolationism and to adopt a policy of open imperialism instead. According to its advocates, such imperialism was justified on strategic, economic, religious, and even emotional grounds.

Behind this outward urge the gradual elimination of frontiers within the United States can be detected. Up to this time, much of the country's energy, both moral and physical, had been channeled toward the internal development of the country, especially along the western frontier. But by 1890, the western frontier had ceased to exist, according to the Census Bureau; it is no mere coincidence that about this time there was a surge in American imperialist ambitions.

Efforts now turned increasingly to endeavors outside the country's continental limits. Under the circumstances, it could only be a matter of time before the U.S. Army and the Navy were called to support and protect American interests overseas.

Seen at the New York Naval Review of 1889, this is the U.S.S. *Chicago*, a 4,500-ton protected cruiser that was launched on December 5, 1885. The ship was authorized in 1883 and completed in 1889. Although it was designed as a commerce raider, it was too slow for this job with a speed of only 18 knots.

"Manifest destiny" was the concept of the moral right of Americans to occupy North America from ocean to ocean. A new concept of this destiny became evident in the late 1870s as American business interests expanded their horizons into the Caribbean and Pacific. There had already been moves in these directions, but they were accelerated by the growth in numbers and capabilities of steam-powered American merchant ships. American commerce boomed during the period. Such trade inevitably needed the support of the Navy, and the government thus found it necessary to build up a network of fuelling stations.

In the years following the Civil War, the concept of "manifest destiny" had convinced many Americans that British North America should become part of the United States. In 1867, the purchase of Alaska eliminated the Russians as competition in North America. It also offered two other advantages: American possession of Alaska was seen as a "finger pointed at Asia"; and it opened a back door into British North

America. American imperialists believed that, by encircling of these possessions, the U.S. could ultimately force British North America to amalgamate with the United States.

"Manifest Destiny" Forestalled in Canada

To foil these American ambitions, the British moved to make its North American possessions into a self-governing dominion. The British North America Act of 1867 established the core of a Canadian federation, which was completed by the purchase of Rupert's Land from the Hudson's Bay Company in 1869, and the accession of Manitoba in 1870 and British Columbia in 1871. Tensions between Britain and the U.S. stemming from the Civil War and the creation of Canada were ended by the Treaty of Washington in 1871.

U.S. trade turned away from Canada and looked toward Asia for rapid growth. While Alaska was recognized as a potentially important link with the Orient, in the

The inauguration of President William McKinley on March 4, 1897, ushered in a new era for the United States, which began to emerge as a real global power with territorial possessions outside the continental boundaries.

William McKinley
For further references see pages
8, 12, 14, 47, 61, 67, 73, 76, 79, 82, 93

short term, trans-Pacific shipping was the only practical way of trading with the Far East and Australasia. At the same time, merchant ships could sweep up the trade potential of the Pacific islands, most notably importing copra for making rope and matting.

The logical stepping stone in the development of trade across the Pacific from the middle of the 19th century was the Polynesian kingdom of the Hawaiian Islands. Here three-power rivalry between the United States, France, and the United Kingdom kept American relations with Hawaii in a state of continual flux. However, in 1867 the United States sidestepped this problem temporarily by annexing the island of Midway. Well to the northwest of Hawaii, it was an ideal stop on the trade route across the central Pacific toward Korea, Japan, China, the Spanish-possessed Philippine Islands, and south-east Asia.

This move did not mean the end of American interest in the Hawaiian Islands, however, which offered far better long-term prospects than Midway. In 1875 the signing of a commercial treaty made the islands virtually an American protectorate, and in 1887 the United States secured rights to Pearl Harbor on Oahu Island as a fueling station and future naval base. In 1893 a new Hawaiian government threatened to cancel these concessions. Supported by American officials, U.S. residents (mainly Honolulu businessmen and sugar planters) overthrew the native monarchy, declared Hawaii a republic, and agitated for American annexation. This pressure was resisted by the second administration of President Grover Cleveland, but the inauguration of President William McKinley in March 1897 opened the way for a period of American expansion. In 1898 the islands were annexed by the United States.

This advance into the central Pacific was given a measure of moral justification by the Spanish-American War, and was completed by the annexation of Wake Island in 1899.

Fueling Station in Samoa

The other main destination for Pacific trade was Australasia, where Australia and New Zealand were beginning to provide exciting prospects. The trade route to these important parts of the British empire ran southwest across the South Pacific. In 1878 the United States secured the right to build and maintain a fueling station at Pago Pago on Tutuila, one of the islands of Samoa. Such was the importance of these islands on the South Pacific trade routes, however, that in 1889 the United States signed a tripartite treaty with the United Kingdom and Germany to recognize their independence and to agree spheres of influence for the U.S. (Tutuila and the Manua groups slightly to the east), the U.K. (Upolu), and Germany (Savaii). Even so, friction between the powers continued, and in 1899 a new treaty partitioned the islands, with Tutuila and the Manuas becoming the American possession of Eastern Samoa.

During the same period, the United States sought to extend its influence in the Caribbean, but with less success. The Navy failed in its efforts to secure fueling stations, but it, and the general public, watched with considerable interest the unsuccessful efforts of private companies to build a canal across the isthmus of Panama. Such a canal would remove the need for ships to sail from the Atlantic and Caribbean around Cape Horn at the tip of South America to reach the Pacific coast and Asia.

So it was a combination of strategic and commercial interests that contributed most significantly to the development of the country's new manifest destiny in its earlier stages. In its later stages, however, the major spur to American expansionism was a humanitarian concern against oppression, especially by the ruling Spanish over the people of Cuba. The commercial and strategic importance of this large island, lying in the entrance to the Gulf of Mexico and stretching southeast into the Caribbean, had already attracted the attention of early expansionists. Yet they were only a small minority of Americans, and only when the Cubans rebelled against their oppressors did most Americans devote any real thought to the island.

Private, Infantry, U.S. Army, Cuba and the Philippines, 1898

This soldier is typical of the enlisted men who served in the Cuban and Philippine campaigns. The combination of light blue trousers with suspenders, dark blue woolen shirts, gaiters, and a brownish hat was standard. There was also a khaki uniform, which would have been better for operations in hot climates, but it was not generally available until after the end of the two campaigns. The weapon is the M1898 Krag-Jorgensen bolt-action rifle.

The war against Spain was greeted with great enthusiasm by most Americans, and volunteers flocked to the colors. These freshly recruited men, still wearing their civilian clothes, are learning the rudiments of army drill.

Rebellion in Cuba

This was certainly the case in 1868, when the Cubans launched a rebellion generally known as the Ten Years' War, the time it took the Spanish to crush the uprising. The Cuban effort to throw off Spanish rule attracted great American sympathy, and some aid, including the sale to a Cuban group of the former Confederate blockade runner *Virginius*. Ironically, the ship captured in October 1873 off Morant Bay, Jamaica, by the Spanish screw corvette *Tornado*, was herself built as a Confederate commerce raider.

While conceding the need to change the way they governed Cuba, but steadily failing to implement any such changes, the Spanish administration maintained a policy of great severity. Cuban discontent simmered, and in February 1895 the suspension of constitutional guarantees brought matters to a head. Open rebellion was sparked by the arrival by sea of insurgent forces from Costa Rica and Santo Domingo. The Spaniards launched a campaign of bitter retaliation, which was unsuccessful in crushing the rebellion, which soon settled into a campaign between 8,000 rebels and perhaps 50,000 Spanish troops initially. The war was initially confined mainly to Oriente Province in eastern Cuba, but soon spread to all parts of the island.

Many Americans demanded intervention, but the Cleveland administration was already involved in a border dispute in Venezuela with one European power, the British. The government refused to intervene, which left the Spanish with a free hand. When their initial measures had failed to crush the Cuban insurrection after 12 months, they resorted to harsher measures implemented by a new Captain-General of Cuba, Valeriano Weyler.

In the closing stages of the 19th century, the Hawaiian Islands began to become increasingly important to the United States as trade extended into and across the Pacific Ocean. The islands therefore became an important coaling station for American merchant ships and the warships that would have to protect them in times of conflict. These Hawaiian cowboys were photographed at Waimea in 1899.

This able soldier arrived in Havana in February 1896 with additional troops. Weyler quickly decided that the only realistic way to defeat the rebels was a policy of isolation in which the island would be divided by *trochas*. These were lines of barbed wire entrenchments and, in the narrowest parts of the island, blockhouses. They confined the rebel forces in specific areas which could then be swept in search-and-destroy operations. At the same time, Weyler organized a policy of *reconcentrado*, in which women, children, and the old were herded from the countryside into detention camps and garrison towns. This policy was effective in the purely military sense, as it deprived the rebels of support in the countryside, caused the deaths of many thousands of people from starvation and disease in the appalling, badly administered camps.

The Power of the Press

These twin policies swayed the tide of the military campaign toward the Spanish but inflamed public opinion in the United States. "Yellow journalism" had become acceptable, and popular newspapers made much of the cruelty of the Spanish policy in Cuba. Weyler was depicted as an inhuman butcher using tactics of the utmost savagery to suppress high-minded patriots fighting only to secure basic freedom from the oppression of an old-fashioned but highly authoritarian European power. The emergence of this newspaper-led antagonism to Spanish policies in Cuba coincided with popular sentiment, and in 1896 both houses of Congress adopted resolutions urging that the United States confer the status of "belligerents" on the Cuban rebels, and at

the same time use its international influence to persuade Spain to grant Cuban independence. Politicians saw the Cuban insurrection as a way of gaining support in the 1896 elections. Others saw the situation as a chance for the United States to secure a naval base in Cuba and so open the Caribbean to American economic and political penetration. Cleveland had not wanted war with Spain, and neither did the new president. In his inaugural speech of March 1897, McKinley said that "We want no wars of conquest; we must avoid the temptation of territorial aggression." However, the Republican platform on which McKinley had won the 1896 election committed the president to use the nation's "influences and good offices to restore peace and give independence" to Cuba. Despite steadily growing political, public, and press pressures for war, McKinley tried patiently to find a diplomatic solution, one that would meet the demands of the Cuban rebels but avoid war between the United States and Spain. At one time, McKinley even offered an American purchase of the island for $300,000,000. The United States demanded that Weyler be replaced; in the spring of 1897, Spain agreed, though Weyler did not in fact return home until October of that year.

In February 1898 there was serious rioting in Havana, and *The New York Journal* secured and published a private letter written by the Spanish minister in Washington to a Spanish editor traveling in the United States. The letter condemned McKinley's December 1897 message to Congress and expressed the minister's opinion that the president was "weak and a bidder for admiration of the crowd ... a would-be politician who tries to leave a door open behind himself while trying to keep on good terms with the jingoes in his party." This slur on the president was too much for most Americans, even though the Spanish minister resigned as a consequence, and American indignation with Spanish policies in Cuba reached a new pitch of anger. Yet McKinley was determined that such an essentially private matter should not lead the country into war and was

inclined to accept the Spanish apologies that had been demanded.

The *Maine* Incident

At this point, fate intervened. At the urging of the American consul in Havana, the administration had reluctantly sent the battleship U.S.S. *Maine* to Cuba on a "courtesy" visit, though the real reason was to protect American citizens in Cuba if necessary. Lying at anchor in Havana harbor, the *Maine* was destroyed by a huge explosion on February 15, 1898, with the loss of 260 lives. A naval investigation committee was appointed by the president. On March 25, this committee announced that the explosion had been external, suggesting to all Americans that the ship had been sunk by the Spanish.

McKinley again refused to rush into hasty action, and on March 27 he sent to Madrid a plan for the peaceful solution

The event that finally sparked the Spanish-American War of 1898 was the destruction of the battleship U.S.S. *Maine* in Havana harbor. The cause was almost certainly a pair of accidental internal explosions, but popular dislike and distrust of the Spaniards meant that most people insisted that the cause was a Spanish submarine mine.

U.S.S. *Maine*
For further references see pages
13, 14

Above: The wreck of the *Maine* in 1911. The wreck was raised in February 1912 and sunk at sea during the following month.

Left: Shortly before her untimely end, the *Maine* enters Havana harbor. This early American battleship was authorized in 1886, launched on November 18, 1890, and completed only in 1895 because of late delivery of the armor. The ship, basically an enlarged copy of the Brazilian *Riachuelo*, displaced 6,682 tons. Originally barque-rigged on three masts, the ship had the mizzen mast removed in 1892.

THE SPANISH BRUTE
ADDS MUTILATION TO MURDER.

Above: A cartoon of the Spanish-American War reveals the strength of popular opinion against the Spaniards, here accused of mutilating the bodies of American soldiers as well as murdering the sailors lost with the *Maine*.

Left: Captain Charles D.Sigsbee of the *Maine*.

of the Cuban problem. Only four days later, the Spanish replied, agreeing to end the policy of *reconcentrado* and to arbitrate the *Maine* disaster, but evading the issue of granting of an armistice to the rebels, and also refusing to promise eventual Cuban independence or to accept McKinley's offer of mediation.

Despite this discouraging response, McKinley still did not admit defeat and moved only slowly toward war, always leaving the possibility open for last-minute negotiation. Twice, McKinley postponed his war message to Congress, but with most sectors of American opinion now firmly committed to war, the president finally had to follow. On April 11, 1898, the president's war message was finally delivered to Congress. Eight days later, both houses passed a joint resolution affirming the independence of Cuba and authorizing the president to take all measures necessary to expel the Spanish from the island. It is interesting to note, however, that the resolution contained an amendment, proposed by Senator Teller of Colorado, forbidding any American annexation of the island.

The Spanish-American War (1898)

McKinley was now committed and acted with considerable speed to order an immediate naval blockade of Cuba. A squadron of warships promptly took up position off Havana. On April 25 Congress declared that a state of war had existed between the United States and Spain since April 21.

So the Spanish-American War, which both Cleveland and McKinley had tried so hard to avoid, began. The declaration of war found the United States badly prepared for military operations, despite the fact that military action had been on the cards for several months and had indeed been mooted for the previous two years.

This overall lack of military preparedness differed to a marked degree in the two major services. In the ten years leading up to the Spanish-American War, the U.S. Navy had achieved considerably more than the U.S. Army, partly because of the navy's strong corps of professional

The Gatling gun had been considerably improved and lightened since the Civil War, but it is a telling indication of the lack of public order during the period that such a weapon is seen here in the hands of a policeman.

officers, and in part from the efforts of career naval officers such as Rear Admiral Stephen B. Luce and Captain Alfred T. Mahan, who were supported by able administrators such as Benjamin Tracy, Secretary of the Navy in the administration of President Benjamin Harrison.

The highly professional capabilities of the navy's more senior officers resulted from the creation in 1885 of the Naval

War College at Newport, Rhode Island, at the instigation of Luce. The college played a major part in developing higher command skills and strategic thinking based on the classic doctrines of sea power evolved by Mahan. These men were able to capitalize on the needs of growing overseas trade at a time of relative prosperity to extract large funds from Congress. This high level of funding had allowed the navy to undertake a program of major construction and modernization to create the so-called New Navy, which got off to a slow start, but later developed considerable momentum.

During the Civil War, the Navy had grown greatly through new construction and the purchase of commercial vessels. Most of these ships were seen as superfluous after the war and therefore discarded. Thus, the strength of the navy weakened as the country relaxed from the pressure of the Civil War and turned its

Left: Men of the U.S. Marine Corps practice bayonet fighting on board their ship, the battleship U.S.S. *Iowa*, on her way to Cuba during the Spanish-American War.

Below Left: Conditions for the soldiers shipped to Cuba were primitive, but were considered acceptable for this short passage. These are sleeping quarters, with side-by-side pairs of bunks stacked three deep.

attention toward matters such as the settling of the West. Congress refused to appropriate funds to construct new ships, and existing ships fell into states of considerable disrepair for lack of adequate maintenance funds. To maintain even the semblance of combat capability, the navy was reduced to secretly rebuilding the ships under the guise of repairs to produce new vessels that retained only the name of their predecessors.

By the early 1880s, most of the navy's ships were obsolete. Most people thought that the navy's main strength lay with its ironclad monitors, which had been revolutionary when they were first placed in service in 1862. Now, though, they were old, small, weak, and poorly suited to anything but coastal defense. They were in general armed with obsolete smooth-bore guns lacking the range, accuracy, and penetrating power of current rifled guns. Their protective armor plates, ineffective against modern projectiles, laid over timbers that were now rotten, as they were still green when they had been built into the ships. The situation was no better with the navy's cruising ships: some had been built before the Civil War without armor plate and with only short-range guns, while others built during and after the Civil War were obsolete by comparison with foreign cruisers offering superior performance and firepower.

In 1881 the situation had become so bad that Secretary of the Navy William H. Hunt appointed a committee, chaired by Rear Admiral John Rogers II, to report on the state of the navy. The committee reported that the U.S. Navy ranked only twelfth in the world, and behind the navies of China, Chile, and Denmark. The seagoing navy of the time was made up of one frigate cruiser, 14 screw sloops, 20 second-class sloops, and four gunboats, all but the last made of wood and all needing repair. The coastal forces included 14 single-turret monitors that had been out of commission for 15 years, and five twin-turret monitors still being built after years of leisurely and interrupted construction since 1874.

The committee recommended that 38 cruisers and 25 torpedo boats should be

built immediately. This was altogether too expensive and revolutionary for Congress to accept. So William E. Chandler, Hunt's successor, was able to begin his construction program for the new navy with just three cruisers and one despatch boat. At the same time, Congress banned the repair of any wooden ship whose overhaul would cost more than 20 percent of the purchase price of a new vessel of the same type and size. This led to the immediate disposal of 46 ships.

The New Navy

The first of the New Navy ships were ordered in 1883, but the accelerating pace of the program meant that, up to 1898, some 110 ships (including six battleships, two protected cruisers, 13 cruisers, and numerous gunboats and torpedo boats) were ordered. Thus the fleet disposition of the U.S. Navy in May 1898, just after the beginning of the Spanish-American War, was in four effective squadrons. The North Atlantic Squadron included the U.S.S. *New York* (flagship), *Indiana, Iowa, Puritan, Amphitrite, Terror, Detroit, Cincinnati, Marblehead, Montgomery*, and *Dolphin*. The Flying Squadron contained the U.S.S. *Brooklyn, Massachusetts, Texas, Minneapolis, Columbia, New Orleans*, and *Scorpion*. The Asiatic Squadron included U.S.S. *Olympia* (flagship), *Baltimore, Raleigh, Petrel, Concord, Boston*, and *McCulloch*. The Pacific Squadron included the *Mohican, Monadnock, Monterey, Philadelphia, Wheeling, Bennington*, and *Albatross*. Finally, there was the U.S.S. *Oregon*, which was *en route* from the Pacific Squadron to the Atlantic Squadron.

The army was not in such a fortunate position. During the previous 25 years, its average strength was about 26,000 officers and men; at the outbreak of the Spanish-American War, it numbered 28,183. Most of this strength was scattered across the country in company and battalion-sized packets. Individual infantrymen and cavalrymen were well trained, competently skilled in minor

A contemporary illustration highlights some of the major elements in American naval power in the waters around Cuba during the 1898 campaign. By contrast with these American ships, the Spanish warships were both obsolescent and lacking in serviceability.

tactics, and good marksmen with the new Krag-Jorgensen rifle. This was an adequate weapon in 30-inch caliber which fired a smokeless cartridge, but it was let down by its cumbersome, five-round sidebox magazine, which had to be loaded with single cartridges at a time when most European nations were already using clip-loaded vertical magazines.

Because of its standard peacetime deployment all over the United States, the army had been unable to train and practice maneuvers in forces larger than the regiment. To make matters worse, it was hard to gather these scattered units together, as the army lacked an overall mobilization plan. Even when the units had been gathered for the creation of brigades and divisions, the army lacked the command staff and the combined organizational and tactical skills to make effective use of such formations. In addition, there was no experience or concept for undertaking joint operations with the navy.

Actual numbers of men in the field could have been bolstered by the National Guard, over 100,000 men strong.

Admittedly, these men lacked the tactical skills of their regular counterparts, and in a fashion calculated to add to American logistical problems, most National Guardsmen still used the Springfield rifle firing a black powder cartridge. Even so, the National Guard might have been useful in Cuba fighting alongside the regular army. But there were several factors that made it difficult to send National Guard units to overseas theaters at short notice. The National Guard organization varied from state to state, and most National Guard units had a deep-seated objection to serving under regular army officers. More significantly, it was not clear under existing law whether or not it was legal to send National Guard units to fight outside the United States.

The Department of War therefore planned to create a new force of federal volunteers under officers appointed by the president, but this move was strongly opposed by the National Guard. Compromise was inevitable. The Mobilization Act, passed by Congress on April 22, 1898, ordained a wartime force of regular and volunteer units grouped into brigades, divisions, and corps. This act

Nelson A. Miles
For further references
see pages
20, 29, 51, 56

also allowed some whole National Guard units to serve: if enough men from a state unit came forward together, they were kept together as a federal volunteer unit.

Too Large an Army

The act called for 125,000 volunteers, but the popularity of the war soon forced Congress to increase this total to 200,000 and to authorize extra special volunteer forces, including the so-called Immunes, 10,000 men from the southern states, who therefore supposedly "possessed immunity from diseases incident to tropical climates."

At the same time, Congress authorized a regular establishment of 65,000 men, more than twice the existing figure. By

the end of the Spanish-American War in August 1898, the strength of the army stood at 275,000 men, including 59,000 regulars and 216,000 volunteers.

The regular army had to leave part of its current strength in the west in case of renewed trouble with the Indians, but it needed larger forces for operations in Cuba. About 25,000 rebels were under arms and were generally considered to be of little real fighting value, though important for scouting and security purposes.

Major General Nelson A. Miles, the commanding general of the army, thought that 80,000 trained men would be enough to take Cuba from the Spanish. Ultimately, the army needed more than three times that many, which imposed a terrible burden on the army's planners, who lacked not only the

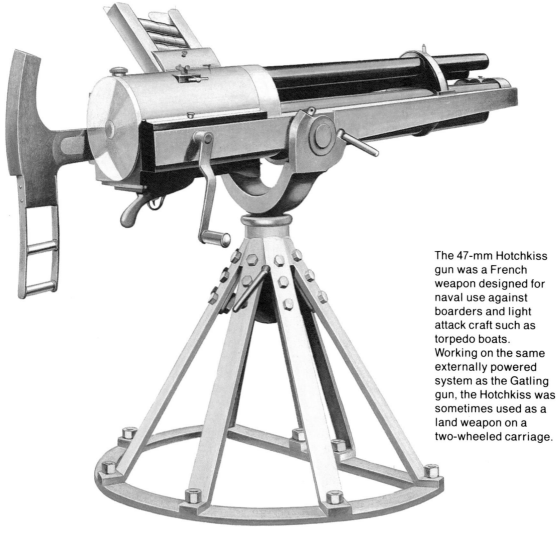

The 47-mm Hotchkiss gun was a French weapon designed for naval use against boarders and light attack craft such as torpedo boats. Working on the same externally powered system as the Gatling gun, the Hotchkiss was sometimes used as a land weapon on a two-wheeled carriage.

19

Tampa
For further references
see pages
29, 31, 33

necessary hardware, but also_ the organization and production machinery to create it. There was confusion at every administrative level. Severe epidemics broke out in several camps, and the whole situation was worsened by the apparent delight of the press in pointing out the mistakes that did, in certain cases, reach quite scandalous proportions.

The situation was complicated still further by disputes about the way in which mobilization should be carried out, and then the basic strategy that should be followed. This problem was compounded by a lack of accurate maps or accurate intelligence about the strength and disposition of the Spanish troops in Cuba.

Lack of Overall Strategic Planning

Overall strategic planning therefore seemed to alter day by day. The agreed basic plan called for a naval blockade of the island while rebel forces continued their campaign of harassment against the Spanish, who were well armed and supplied with other modern equipment. The American planners did not appreciate, however, that the Spanish in Cuba were short of ammunition and other basic supplies, and that their senior commanders were generally incompetent and pessimistic.

Supporters of this naval grand strategy, including Mahan, believed that the blockade would eventually force the Spanish to surrender as their supplies ran out and their morale crashed. The clear advantage was that this strategy avoided any direct clash between American and Spanish ground forces; the latter would arrive in Cuba as occupation forces only after the Spanish had surrendered.

In line with this plan, Miles proposed to assemble, equip, and train his 80,000-man force around the nucleus of the available regular army units. Miles believed that there would be enough time to train his force while the naval blockade took effect, sapping the determination and supplies of the Spanish. He also believed that no landing should be undertaken before the end of the unhealthy rainy season in October. As a

first step, Miles planned to concentrate regular army units in Chickamauga Park, Georgia, for intensive training in combined-arms operations. This experience would be necessary in any Cuban operation, but had been impossible to practice earlier because the regular army was so widely dispersed.

This sensible – and wholly practical – strategic plan did not fit the mood of the American public, which wanted immediate action against the Spanish. As a result, Secretary of War Russell M. Alger, who had been a general in the Civil War, overruled Miles and ordered the infantry regiments of the regular army to assemble instead at New Orleans, Mobile, and Tampa. All these ports on the Gulf of Mexico could be used as launching points for an invasion of Cuba. Some infantry regiments did in fact go to Chickamauga Park later, where they were able to undertake combined-arms training with the cavalry and artillery regiments of the regular establishment.

At this point, the politically motivated decision to create a large volunteer force came home to roost. It seriously compromised the army's plans when much of its administrative effort was devoted to equipping, supplying, and training the many thousands of volunteers who flooded into reception areas. These bases were located in the southern states so the men would be fairly close to their embarkation points to help them acclimatize to the climate in Cuba. Some of these volunteers had militia experience, but most were completely raw.

Their first taste of military life cured the volunteers of most of their enthusiasm. In the reception camps, they found that much essential equipment (including such basics as underwear, socks, shoes, and even rifles) was lacking, food was in short supply and very badly prepared even when it was available, sanitary facilities were appalling, and medical services were swamped. Training of the volunteers was further hampered by a lack of effective volunteer officers.

Even when these failings were highlighted in the newspapers, red tape, combined with poor management skills, thwarted all efforts to remedy the situation. The sole department to emerge with

Officer, 1st Volunteer Cavalry Regiment (The Rough Riders), Cuba, 1898

The complete uniform was made of khaki cotton, and the shirt had a yellow collar with gilt regimental devices and yellow shoulder tabs carrying shoulder strap rank insignia. The polka dot bandana favored by Lieutenant Colonel Theodore Roosevelt became the trademark of The Rough Riders. The khaki uniform was worn by many other officers in the Cuban campaign and proved so successful and popular that it was standardized in 1899.

any measure of credit from this trying time was the Ordnance Department.

The inefficiency that made the life of the volunteers so miserable was also evident in the War Department's planning and implementation of operations. Congress had provided no peacetime apparatus for coordinating military capability with foreign policy requirements. In addition, the United States entered the war without any real grand strategic plan, and without the staff and intelligence apparatus even to undertake realistic operational planning. In April 1898 the army was faced with an amphibious assault on an enemy shore after a sea crossing. This is one of the most difficult and hazardous military undertakings there is, and both the War Department and the high command of the army found themselves unprepared. There were capable men in both organizations who could probably have come up with a workable, effective plan in due course. But time was a limited

commodity since political pressures and public opinion demanded an immediate invasion of Cuba.

As it turned out, the decisive operations of the Spanish-American War fell to the navy, which was much better prepared to accept the burden. Even so, last-minute alterations in its strategic plan to deal with the Spanish navy threatened to reduce its overall effectiveness.

Rumor Sweeps the East Coast

Soon after the American declaration of war, it was rumored that a Spanish fleet under Admiral Pascual Cervera Topete was sailing from Spain toward the Atlantic coast of the United States, and a thoroughly alarmed public screamed for naval protection of this seaboard. The Navy Department therefore removed some of the best fighting ships from Rear Admiral William T. Sampson's North Atlantic Squadron, which had been allo-

Dewey's approach to the Philippines before the battle of Manila Bay.

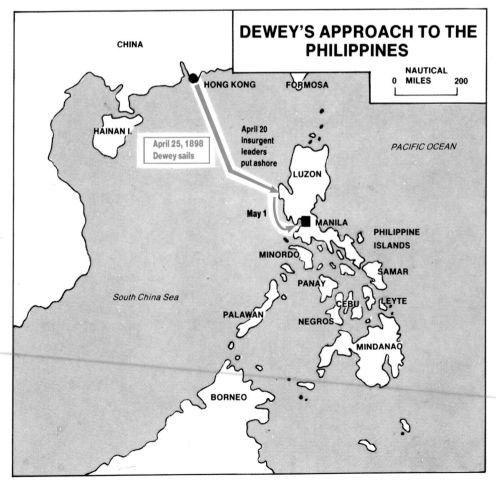

Marines and seamen drawn up for inspection aboard U.S.S. *Essex*.

cated the task of blockading Cuba. These ships were used to create the Flying Squadron under Commodore Winfield S. Schley, whose task was to maintain a watch for Cervera off the eastern coast of the United States. Right at the beginning of the war, therefore, the Navy Department altered its own strategic scheme, based on Mahan's teachings, to concentrate its eastern forces in a single fleet to operate in the Caribbean against Spanish naval reinforcement of Cuba.

In the Pacific theater, the Navy Department stuck to the latest form of its overall plan, which had only been completed in 1897. Developed since 1895 by officers at the Naval Staff College in collaboration with the Office of Naval Intelligence, the plan called for a naval descent on the Philippines to destroy all Spanish warships, capture Manila, and blockade all major ports. The objective of this plan was to weaken Spain by cutting her important revenues from the Philippines, and to provide the United States

with a bargaining counter in the eventual peace negotiations, when the United States would be able to offer Spain the return of the Philippines in exchange for its departure from Cuba.

The navy had started active preparations for war in January 1898 under the impetus of Acting Secretary of the Navy Theodore D. Roosevelt, replacing Secretary of the Navy John D. Long who was in poor health. Roosevelt telegraphed to all commanders, instructing them to ready their forces for war against Spain. Commodore George Dewey in the Pacific was instructed to gather his Asiatic Squadron in the British colony of Hong Kong, where it would be handily placed for a descent on the Philippines after taking on coal and other supplies. On April 24, therefore, Dewey was fully prepared to implement the attack on the Philippines on the day that he received his orders. The American naval commander had used his time in Hong Kong most effectively. In addition to preparing his ships and men,

Dewey's flagship in the Battle of Manila Bay was U.S.S. *Olympia*, a protected cruiser originally planned for commerce raiding. Displacing 5,586 tons, the *Olympia* was authorized in 1888, launched on November 5, 1892, and completed in 1895. With two reciprocating steam engines delivering 13,500 horsepower to two shafts, the ship could achieve the notably high speed of 20 knots. Her armament was four 8-inch guns in two twin turrets, 10 5-inch guns. 14 6-pounder guns, and six 18-inch torpedo tubes; her crew was 410.

he had made a complete study of the Spanish forces in the Philippines and was completely confident that his force could destroy the Spanish squadron in the islands. Dewey had also made contact with Emilio Aguinaldo, the leader of the main Filipino independence movement.

The United States was now at war, and in accordance with international law, the British ordered the American squadron to leave Hong Kong by April 25. The Asiatic Squadron sailed that day, anchoring in nearby Chinese waters until April 27, when two Filipino leaders arrived. Dewey then sailed for the Philippines and put the two rebel leaders ashore on the west coast of Luzon during April 30. Sailing south to Subic Bay, the main Spanish naval base on the western side of the Bataan peninsula, Dewey discovered that the Spanish squadron was not there. He pressed ahead into Manila Bay past the coastal defense batteries on Corregidor and El Fraile islands in the mouth of the bay.

The Battle of Manila Bay

The Asiatic Squadron spotted the Spanish squadron off Cavite, just south

of Manila, early in the morning of May 1. The line of American ships was headed by Dewey's flagship *Olympia* followed by another cruiser, the *Baltimore*, the gunboat *Petrel*, the cruiser *Raleigh*, the gunboat *Concord*, the cruiser *Boston*, and a revenue cutter. Lying at anchor, Admiral Patricio Montojo's squadron included one modern cruiser and the elderly cruisers and gunboats.

In a line running southwest from the Spanish flagship, the *Reina Christina*, were the *Castilla, Isla de Cuba, Isla de Luzon, Don Antonio de Uloa, Don Juan de Austria, Marques del Duero, General Lezo*, and *Velasco*, with the *Argos* and *El Cano* lying closer inshore. The ships were all lying at anchor, and their guns were supplemented by three coast-defense guns, one of 120-mm caliber and the other two of 150-mm caliber.

The American squadron ran south through the fire of the Spanish batteries protecting Manila (two 120mm, four 140mm, two 150mm, and four 240-mm

guns), and once the Spanish ships were within range, they opened fire at 5:48 a.m. to begin the Battle of Manila Bay. The American ships circled seaward of the Spanish ships as they fired, and the first phase of the gunnery duel lasted until 7:35 a.m., when Dewey broke off the action after he had been informed mistakenly that ammunition was running short.

The break allowed the Americans to take stock of the situation, count casualties, and eat a leisurely breakfast before resuming the battle at 11:16 a.m. By this time, the smoke of the battle's first phase had cleared, revealing that the Spanish squadron was in poor shape. The *Christina* and *Castilla* had been sunk, and most of the surviving ships were badly damaged. For another three hours, the American ships pounded their stationary targets, which were all sunk or put out of action. The Spanish lost 381 men killed or wounded, while the only American casualties were eight of the

The Battle of Manila Bay was a completely one-sided battle in which the anchored and completely inferior Spanish ships were outgunned by the American warships. Yet the destruction of the Spanish fleet was essential to American success in the Philippines, since it eliminated any chance for the Spaniards to cut the American lines of communication or hinder operations on land.

The naval Battle of Manila Bay occurred on 1 May, 1898. The American Commodore George Dewey reported:

"The squadron then proceeded to the attack, the flagship Olympia under my personal direction, leading, followed at a distance by the Baltimore, Raleigh, Petrel, Concord and Boston, in the order named, which formation was maintained throughout the action. The squadron opened fire at nineteen minutes to six A.M. While advancing to the attack two mines were exploded ahead of the flagship too far to be effective.

"The squadron maintained a continuous and precise fire, at ranges carrying from 5,000 to 2,000 yards, counter-marching in a line approximately parallel to that of the Spanish fleet. The enemy's fire was vigorous, but generally ineffective.

Quite early in the engagement the two launches put out towards the Olympia with the apparent intention of using torpedoes. One was sunk and the other disabled by our fire and beached before an opportunity occurred to fire torpedoes.

"At seven A.M. the Spanish flagship Reina Christina made a desperate attempt to leave the line and come out to engage at short range, but was received with such galling fire, the entire battery of the Olympia being concentrated upon her, that she was barely able to return to the shelter of the point. Fires started in her by our shells at this time were not extinguished until she sank.

"The three batteries at Manila had kept up a continuous fire from the beginning of the engagement, which fire was not returned by this squadron. The first of these batteries was situated on the south mole head, at the entrance to the Pasig River; the second on the south bastion of the walled city of Manila, and the third at Malate, about one-half mile further south. At this point I sent a message to the Governor General to the effect that if the batteries did not cease firing the city would be shelled. This had the effect of silencing them.

"At twenty-five minutes to eight A.M. I ceased firing and withdrew the squadron for breakfast. At sixteen minutes past eleven A.M. returned to the attack. By this time the Spanish flagship and almost the entire Spanish fleet were in flames. At half-past twelve P.M. the squadron ceased firing, the batteries being silenced and the ships sunk, burnt and deserted.

"I am unable to obtain complete accounts of the enemy's killed and wounded, but believe their losses to be very heavy. The Reina Christina alone had 150 killed, including the captain, and ninety wounded. I am happy to report that the damage done to the squadron under my command was inconsiderable."

Dewey's opponent, the Spanish Admiral Montojo, reported

"The Americans fired most rapidly. There came upon us numberless projectiles, as the three cruisers at the head of the line devoted themselves almost entirely to fight the Christina, my flag-ship. A short time after the action commenced one shell exploded in the forecastle and put out of action all of those who served the four rapid fire cannon, making splinters of the forward mast, which wounded the helmsman on the bridge, when Lieutenant Jose Nunez took the wheel with a coolness worthy of the greatest commendation, steering until the end of the fight.

In the meanwhile another shell exploded in the orlop, setting fire to the crew's bags, which they were, fortunately, able to control. The enemy shortened the distance between us, and rectifying his aim, covered us with a rain of rapid-fire projectiles.

"At half-past seven one shell destroyed completely the steering gear. I ordered to steer by hand while the rudder was out of action. In the meanwhile another shell exploded on the poop and put out of action nine men. Another destroyed the mizzenmast head, bringing down the flag and my ensign, which were replaced immediately.

''A fresh shell exploded in the officer's cabin, covering the hospital with blood, destroying the wounded who were being treated there. Another exploded in the ammunition room astern, filling the quarters with smoke and preventing the working of the hand-steering gear. As it was impossible to control the fire, I had to flood the magazine when the cartridges were beginning to explode.

''Amidships several shells of smaller caliber went through the smokestack, and one of the large ones penetrated the fire-room, putting out of action one master gunner and twelve men serving the guns. Another rendered useless the starboard bow gun. While the fire astern increased, fire was started forward by another shell, which went through the hull and exploded on the deck.

''The broadside guns, being undamaged, continued firing until there were only one gunner and one seaman remaining unhurt for firing them, as the gun's crews had been frequently called on to substitute those charged with steering, all of whom were out of action.

''The ship being out of control, the hull, smokepipe and masts riddled with shot, half of her crew out of action, among whom were seven officers, I gave the order to sink and abandon the ship before the magazines should explode, making signal at the same time to the Cuba and Luzon to assist in saving the rest of the crew.''

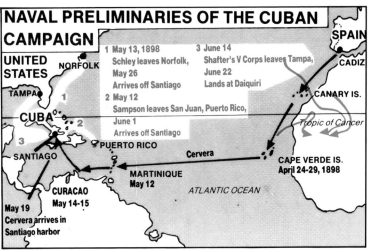

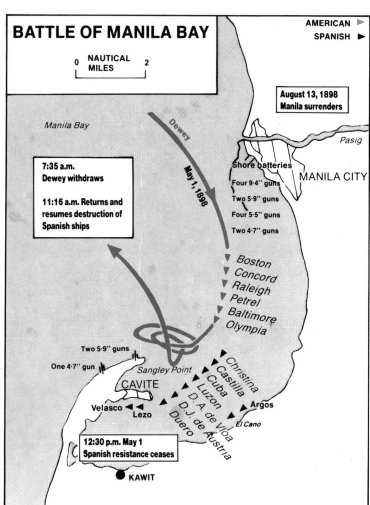

Top: The naval preliminaries of the Cuban campaign.

Above: The Battle of Manila Bay.

The victor of the Battle of Manila Bay, Rear Admiral George W. Dewey, was born in 1837 and died in 1917.

Baltimore's sailors injured by a shell from one of the guns at Cavite. Dewey now ordered the shelling of the batteries at Cavite, and once they had been pounded into submission, the Americans landed and took possession of the peninsula on which Cavite lies. Dewey's total strength of only 1,700 men was wholly inadequate to tackle Manila. The commodore therefore requested the despatch of army forces from the United States. While they were being readied in California and transported to the islands, Dewey ordered a blockade of the city and agreed with the Spanish governor that the shore guns would not fire on the American ships. If they did, a bombardment of Manila was promised.

Land and sea blockade

Until the American land forces arrived, it was important to keep the Spanish pinned in Manila. Dewey therefore gave small arms and other support to the Filipino rebels, who invested the city from the land side and soon spread the rebellion to other islands. Late in May, an American ship brought Aguinaldo from Hong Kong to take command of the rebellion.

A major problem faced by Dewey was

the arrival of British, French, and German naval forces in Manila Bay. Sent on the pretext of protecting their nationals in the islands from excesses by the rebels, these ships were in fact clear evidence that the European powers were not prepared to let a potential power vacuum develop in the islands if the Americans pulled out. The most troublesome of the European commanders was Rear Admiral Otto von Diederichs, but Dewey's firm and patient handling of this German officer prevented any incidents. As soon as the European powers were confident that the Americans were not about to abandon the Philippines, they pulled out their naval forces.

Many thousands of miles to the east, meanwhile, events had been gathering momentum more slowly. Here, in the Caribbean, American naval strength decided the complexion of land operations. During the first part of May, the location of Cervera's Spanish fleet remained a mystery. Until it was discovered, the army could not decide where to undertake any landing in Cuba. Pending the discovery of Cervera's whereabouts, the War Department moved ahead slowly with plans for a landing somewhere near Havana by Miles's expeditionary force, which was being readied at Tampa, Florida.

Cervera reaches Cuba

Cervera had in fact sailed from Cadiz in southern Spain with four armored cruisers, three of them towing torpedo boats. He made slow progress across the Atlantic, hampered by the poor condition of the ships and a shortage of coal. Proceeding via the Canary Islands, Cervera reached the Cape Verde Islands on April 24 and departed only on April 29. The Spanish squadron then crossed the Atlantic to reach the French island pos-

Port Tampa, Florida, as the American expeditionary force embarked for Santiago at the beginning of the Cuban campaign. The concept of combat loading was not well developed at the time, and as a result men and equipment were loaded as they arrived, wherever space could be found. This meant that disembarkation was very disorganized, with the men generally lacking the equipment they needed immediately. Had the Spanish been more acute and more determined, they could probably have pushed the invaders back into the sea.

session of Martinique on May 12. Here the Spanish admiral could not get enough coal for his ships and left for the Dutch island of Curaçao, which he reached on May 14. The same situation prevailed here and, leaving the island on May 15, Cervera decided to seek the safety of Santiago de Cuba, the only unblockaded port in Cuba. The Spanish squadron ran into the harbor under the safety of the guns on May 19.

The presence of Spanish ships was confirmed by Schley's Flying Squadron, which had left Norfolk, Virginia, on May 13. The squadron had sailed south along the American coast, then west past the tip of Florida into the Gulf of Mexico, and finally around the western end of Cuba to arrive off Santiago on May 26. The Navy Department was not sure at first that Schley had in fact discovered Cervera's squadron, and it was only with the arrival of Sampson's North Atlantic Squadron on June 1 that the fact was confirmed. Sampson had been patrolling between Havana and the Puerto Rican port of San Juan. He was at the western end of his

patrol when Schley's news reached him The North Atlantic Squadron immediately turned and, passing around the eastern end of the island, reached Santiago on June 1. Sampson soon relayed the information that Schley was right, and plans were set up to defeat Cervera's squadron and land in Cuba.

Santiago's harbor lies in a large bay whose entrance is only about 400 yards wide and dominated by high ground on each side. On the eastern side lay Morro Castle and two groups of coast-defense guns (the Morro and Estrella batteries); on the western side were the Upper and Lower Socapa batteries. On the inland side of this entrance is a small island, around which the Spanish had sited three groups of remote controlled mines. Finally, any ships that managed to break past these defenses faced a last group of guns (the Punta Gordo battery) on a headland northeast of the island before they could enter the harbor itself. Most of the guns in these fortifications were old muzzleloading weapons, dating from 1688 to 1783, but there were also a few

American soldiers awaiting embarkation relax in a Florida transit camp.

Santiago
For further references
see pages
31, *33*, *34*, 35, *36*, 38, *40*,
43, 44, 47, 48, 50, *51*, 56

William T. Sampson
For further references
see pages
22, *31*, 34, *36*, *47*, 48, 51

Winfield Schley
For further references
see pages
23, 48, 49

Rear Admiral William T. Sampson was the senior officer of the American naval forces operating in the waters around Cuba.

modern guns taken from a cruiser and mounted in the Upper Socapa and Punta Gordo batteries.

Despite the age of the fortifications and the majority of their guns, Sampson found by bitter experience that a naval bombardment could not silence them to make it possible for his ships to enter the harbor. Sampson decided that the best course was to block the harbor entrance by sinking a collier in the channel to bottle up the Spanish squadron. On the night of June 2/3, Lieutenant Richmond P. Hobson and seven volunteers took the *Merrimac* into the entrance and sank her. This gallant effort failed to block the channel, however.

Sampson now decided that he needed the support of land forces to take the batteries. Awaiting the arrival of an army detachment from Florida, the admiral used his marines to seize Guantanamo Bay, east of Santiago, as a forward base. Thus the first land skirmish of the Spanish-American War was a brisk fight as the marines drove off the small Spanish force in the area.

Over-hasty yet slow embarkation

The War Department had organized the army into eight corps, but by the end of May 1898, only Major General William R. Shafter's V Corps was anywhere near ready for action. Receiving Sampson's request for land forces, the War Department decided that the ideal moment had come to follow public opinion. Shafter was instructed on May 31 to embark his men at Tampa, move to Cuba as rapidly as possible, and undertake operations against Santiago in cooperation with the navy.

It took two weeks to embark the corps. There were many reasons for the slow progress of this operation, including lack of any overall embarkation plan and staff,

William R. Shafter
For further references see pages 34, 35, 36, 43, 47, 48, 50, *51*,

31

Major, 2nd Artillery Regiment, U.S. Army, Cuba, 1898

This officer wears the established uniform of the period. The field glasses were an essential adjunct used for locating targets and spotting the fall of fire. The sword is the standard officer's sword, and the belt pistol holster carried the Colt Army Model of 1892.

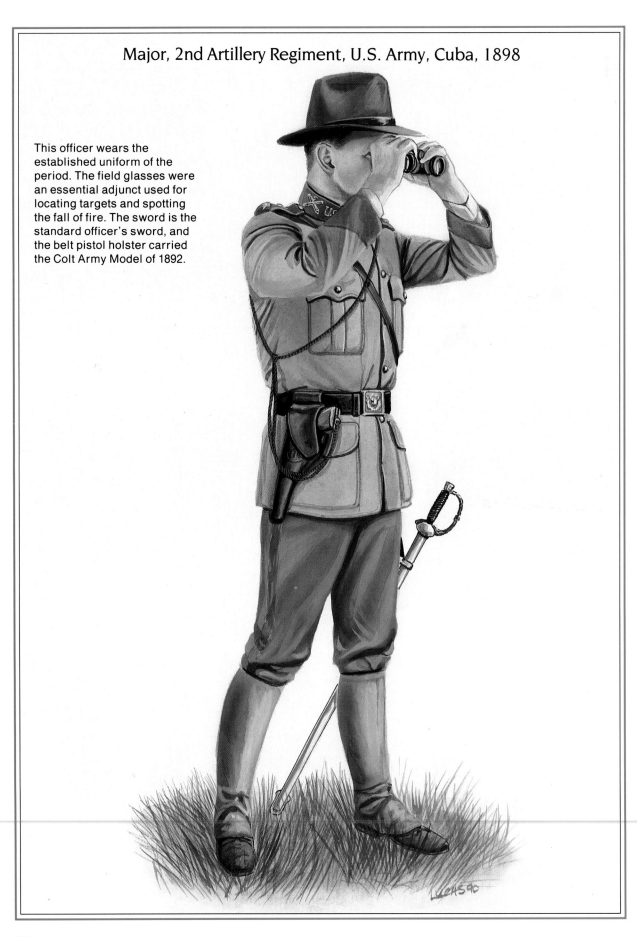

and the poor facilities offered by Tampa as a port. There was only one pier and only a single-track railroad linking Tampa with the rest of the United States. Movement snarl-ups were frequent, the men often had to wait long periods in railroad cars before reaching their ships, and supplies were loaded as they arrived, not according to a plan that took account of unloading priorities for an assault landing. The confusion was great, but eventually the corps was loaded and ready for departure.

The formation had 16,888 men in 18 regular and two volunteer infantry regiments, ten regular and two volunteer

American generals of the Santiago campaign. Major General Leonard Wood became an important U.S. Army Chief of Staff in 1910.

cavalry squadrons in the dismounted role, one mounted cavalry squadron, six batteries of artillery, and one company of Gatling guns organized into two infantry divisions, one under-strength cavalry division, and one independent infantry brigade. The troop convoy sailed on June 14, joined up with its naval escort the following day off the Florida Keys, and reached a point off Santiago on June 20.

When they arrived, there was no agreed plan for the troops' use. As Sampson and Shafter met to discuss such matters, the men and animals on board the transports had to suffer torments of heat, bad food, and unsanitary conditions.

Sampson wanted the troops to land on the eastern side of the harbor entrance and storm up a 230-foot bluff to take Morro Castle and the Morro and Estrella batteries from the rear. Such a move, the naval commander said, would open the bay to his ships, which could then clear the mines, enter the bay, and tackle the Spanish ships. Shafter thought that his lack of heavy artillery would make it impossible to take the castle at the summit of a steep rise. He therefore decided to follow the advice of a rebel leader, General Calixto Garcia, and land at Daiquiri 12 miles to the east. This would allow the men of V Corps to come ashore against minimal opposition, provide a base for subsequent operations, and constitute a jumping-off point for the operational scheme that Shafter had wanted all along, namely an encirclement of Santiago from the east.

The landing at Daiquiri

The landing was ordered for June 22, with diversions created by naval bombardments of Aguadores and Siboney, and by the feint landing of one division at Cabanas, west of the entrance to Santiago Bay. The landing areas were shelled, the troops finally began to land, and no opposition was encountered. Unloading was as confused as the loading in Tampa, especially as many merchant captains refused to bring their chartered ships close inshore. This meant that the landing was slow and hesitant, especially as the navy had no lighters to spare. Many of the horses were dropped into the sea to swim ashore, but many swam out to sea and were lost.

Had the Spanish been able to respond rapidly and firmly, they would have stood a very good chance of driving the Americans back into the sea. By this time, there were more than 200,000 Spanish troops in Cuba, including 36,000 in Santiago province but there was no effort to tackle the landing directly. Thus, 6,000 Americans landed on the first day and the other 11,000 on the following two days. Once ashore, the American soldiers were joined by perhaps 5,000 rebels under Garcia.

Shafter wasted little time before pushing west toward Santiago. On June 23, Brigadier General Henry L. Lawton's advance guard moved along the coast road

Entitled "The Battle of La Guasima, June 24 - The Heroic Stand of the Rough Riders," this illustration helps to highlight one major feature of the Santiago campaign, namely the combination of the rugged terrain and the thickness of the vegetation that often made movement very difficult.

to seize Siboney, which became V Corps' main base of operations on June 24. The same day, the dismounted cavalry of the division commanded by Brigadier General Joseph W. Wheeler, a celebrated Confederate cavalry commander of the Civil War, pushed inland. At Las Guasimas, they encountered the rear gaurd of the Spanish forces pulling back to Santiago. The Spanish had only 1,500 men here, though they could have concentrated about 12,000 in a short time. After checking the 950 dismounted cavalrymen in the so-called Battle of Las Guasimas, the defending Spaniards fell back once more.

Wheeler was an impetuous commander. As senior officer ashore, he took both his own and Lawton's divisions forward to Sevilla. This move put the Americans within five miles of the San Juan Heights overlooking Santiago, but it created a considerably more complicated

supply chain than Shafter had planned. Shafter ordered Wheeler to advance no further, and the next few days were spent in concentrating V Corps and its supplies near Sevilla.

By this time, Shafter had come ashore, and it was soon apparent that heat, humidity, and disease were already affecting his men. The hurricane season was also imminent, and information reached Shafter that some 8,000 Spanish troops were moving south from Holquin to bolster the 28,200 men of General Arsenio Linares's IV Corps for the defense of Santiago. Shafter decided that the only sensible choice was an immediate attack to capture Santiago. The commander of V Corps laid out a simple plan, which depended on an early capture of the dominating San Juan Heights by Brigadier General Jacob F. Kent's 1st Infantry Division on the left and the dismounted

In the Battle of Las Guasimas, a force of about 1,000 dismounted American cavalrymen (the Rough Riders, the 1st Cavalry Regiment, and the 10th Cavalry Regiment) blundered into an ambush laid by about 1,500 retreating Spaniards. Even so, the American force overcame their initial shock and pushed the Spaniards back. U.S. losses were 18 killed, 60 wounded, and nine missing.

Cavalry Division on the right, in all some 8,000 men with support elements. Wheeler was ill, so the Cavalry Division was commanded by Brigadier General Samuel S. Sumner.

The Battle of El Caney

This offensive was scheduled for July 1. As a preliminary move, Lawton's 2nd Infantry Division and a battery of artillery were to clear the American right flank by moving two miles north to take the fortified village of El Caney. This would cut Santiago's water supplies, which flowed from Cuabitas in the north. It would also block the road down which the Spanish reinforcements were reportedly advancing. Shafter thought that the El Caney operation should take about two hours. Afterward, Lawton's division could wheel southwest to take up a position on Wheeler's right as the third division for the main assault, in the process enveloping the northern flank of the Spanish

entrenched defenses on the San Juan Heights and Kettle Hill.

The only other route which the Spaniards could reinforce was the Cobre Road from the northwest. Shafter asked Garcia to block it with his rebel forces. The last components of the offensive were a feint advance along the coast road toward Aguadores by one regiment of an infantry brigade that had just landed at Siboney, and a naval demonstration off the entrance to Santiago harbor.

The overall plan was good, but its implementation proved far more difficult than anyone had expected, largely as a result of poor coordination, very difficult terrain, and the effects of temperature and humidity. One of the main problems was that Shafter, who can be described most charitably as corpulent, was laid low by the heat and had to leave operational control of the Battle of San Juan to others.

Except for open ground at El Caney and the coverless slopes of the San Juan Heights, the battlefield was heavily

El Caney was the key to the northeastern approaches of Santiago; this photograph from Fort Vico emphasizes the roughness of the terrain.
Opposite Top: This illustration of the Battle of El Caney has been foreshortened to get in Santiago and Santiago Bay, together with Cervera's blockaded squadron and Sampson's blockade force.
Opposite Bottom: American field artillery of the period was little more than adequate. Seen here in the background and foreground respectively are a 3-inch field gun and a 47-mm Hotchkiss gun.

wooded. This restricted movement to the area's few roads. The Spanish were well acquainted with the area, and their fixed defenses were sited to gain maximum advantage from the terrain. The defenses themselves were centered on small forts and blockhouses built of stone, and many were covered by barbed wire entanglements.

The first American formation to encounter problems was the 2nd Infantry Division at El Caney. Here the Spanish garrison of 520 men under Brigadier General Joaquin Vara de Ray was well dug in and stubborn. The American guns fired ineffectively at long range, and the black smoke of its outmoded Springfields made the 2nd Massachusetts Regiment so conspicuous that the Spanish, with their modern 7mm Mauser rifles, forced the regiment back, out of the American line. Brigadier General John C. Bate's independent infantry brigade was sent up to reinforce Lawton, bringing the American strength to 6,650 men, but no real progress was made until early afternoon.

The Spanish base was a fort and some stone blockhouses connected by wire entanglements, and it was only as they began to run out of ammunition that the Spanish began to falter. Lawton moved his artillery closer, and shortly after 4:00 p.m., the Americans stormed the fort, killing the heroic Vara de Ray and most of the garrison.

The Battle of San Juan Heights

Farther south, the attack by the 1st Infantry Division and the Cavalry Division, in all some 8,400 men, had started slowly with a confused advance from their overnight bivouac along the road to Santiago. A Signal Corps observation balloon was being towed by this force, and it made an easy aiming point for the Spanish artillery. Two American fieldguns, both obsolete black-powder weapons, tried to support the advance with fire from El Pozo Hill just south of the line of advance, but were quickly forced out of action by the more effective fire of two modern Krupp guns in Spanish hands.

With the advance straggling along, the

The fighting on the edge of Santiago was severe but inconclusive, and Shafter then decided to hold his position and demand the surrender of the city.

Previous Page:
A heavily idealized illustration shows Theodore Roosevelt and the Rough Riders at the Battle of San Juan Hill.

observer in the balloon finally spotted a small but roughly parallel track south of the main road, where Kent diverted part of his division to speed his advance and broaden his front. Kent's leading unit, the 71st New York Regiment, panicked and refused to advance, but was then driven forward by the weight of the regular units behind it.

Eventually, both American divisions took up an irregular line along the San Juan River, roughly southeast of Kettle Hill, due east of San Juan Heights. The American regiments tried to advance up the exposed slopes of the hills leading to the ridge line that was their objective, but they were completely pinned down by the rifle fire of the Spanish infantry. The American position was now becoming dangerous. Ammunition supplies were running short, artillery support had ended, casualty rates were mounting, and communications were virtually nonexistent. It was also clear that no support could be expected from the 2nd Infantry Division, which was still tied up around El Caney.

Gatling gun intervention

At this critical moment of the battle,

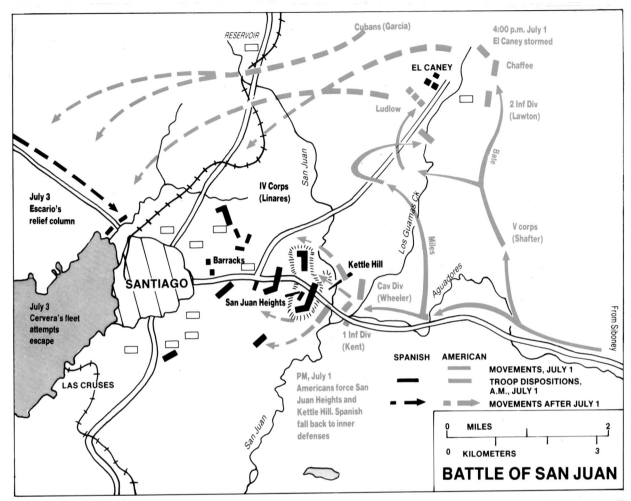

Top: The Battle of San Juan.

Above: The American advance on Santiago.

2nd Lieutenant John H. Parker arrived between the two divisions with his battery of Gatling guns. Parker pushed his guns as far forward as he could and opened a withering fire on the Spanish trenches, whose defenders immediately started to pull back.

It remains unclear who actually ordered the main assault at about 12:00, but at about this time, the Americans stormed forward against the Spanish forward positions. Elements of the Cavalry Division, including the black 9th Cavalry Regiment and part of the black 10th Cavalry Regiment together with Lieutenant Colonel Theodore Roosevelt's "Rough Riders," stormed Kettle Hill. Then men of the 1st Infantry Division, supported by the Gatling guns, stormed San Juan Hill at the southern end of the San Juan Heights, driving the 520-man Spanish force commanded by Vaquero back from their network of blockhouses and wire-covered trenches toward Fort

Above: A composite illustration highlights some of the main episodes of the Spanish-American War.

Right: American soldiers rest before the beginning of the Battle of San Juan Hill in July 1898.

Canosa. Exhausted by the day's movement and fighting, the men of the 1st Infantry Division and the Cavalry Division could not pursue the Spanish as they retired to Fort Canosa, which was the core of the main Spanish defense line.

The 2nd Infantry Division started toward Santiago once it had taken El Caney. Soon after nightfall, however, Lawton's advance guard came under fire near the Ducoureau House, and the American divisional commander sidetracked his formation, as he was unwilling to commit his men to a night action against a force of unknown size in unknown country. Moving back to El Caney and then down to El Pozo Hill, the 2nd Infantry Division finally reached its allotted place on the right of the main force, less than one mile west of the Ducoureau House, at noon on July 2.

The Americans had therefore achieved their main task of the day, but more slowly than anticipated and at the cost of some 1,700 casualties. Shafter's corps held the dominating ground of the San Juan Heights, yet its formations were disorganized and its men thoroughly shaken. Shafter's appreciation of this situation had to take these factors into account. He also had to recognize that the Spanish had been driven only from their outer defense line. They were in fact still firmly sited for the protection of Santiago, in a main defensive position considerably more formidable than the outer line that had just cost the Americans so dear.

On July 2, the arrival of the 2nd Infantry Division allowed the American line to be extended around the north side of Santiago and then southwest virtually to the head of Santiago Bay. Garcia's 4,200-strong rebel forces occupied the heights north of the Cobre Road to prevent the arrival of any Spanish reinforcements.

The trenches of the 7th Infantry Regiment just before the fighting for Santiago. The regiment had been involved in the fighting for El Caney and had since moved into a position just east of the road connecting the city with the Santiago reservoir at Cuabitas. In this position, the regiment also covered the only railroad connecting Santiago with San Luis in the interior of the island.

43

The Americans landed in Cuba on 22 June, 1898. Included in their ranks were the "Rough Riders," a volunteer cavalry force led by Teddy Roosevelt. A young private describes their first combat at La Quasima on 24 June:

"Today we had the first brush with the enemy. We were marching in double file on a path through the woods, when the Spaniards set on us. There was a tremendous popping, and L troop suffered severely. On each side was dense jungle. We charged as skirmishers in the direction where the shooting was. It was awfully hard, as the chaparrel was very thick cactus, overhanging vines and other growths.

"It was about eight A.M., and we had been marching since five, with our heavy rolls and haversacks. We went blindly down a hill. I heard the scream or whirr of bullets, saw dust fly and heard little explosions. I did not see the enemy or smoke, but we fired a couple of rounds in their direction to try our guns. We continued this sort of work for three hours, tramping up and down as fast as we could. The perspiration simply rolled off us, and the boys got reckless and threw off everything but their cartridge belts.

"Mentally, I felt perfectly cool – never more so. Meanwhile, poor L lost Captain Capron, their first lieutenant, Sergeant Hamilton Fish, Jr., and about six others, with seventeen wounded. The Spaniards fled, but not until we lost twenty killed and forty wounded. They ought to have done better with our extended line and their numbers. Poor Marcus Russell, of Albany, was also shot. He enlisted at the same time I did.

"It is a great honor for our regiment to be in the first scrap, and we did as much as any one could do. I threw my roll away with the rest, but noted the spot, and afterward tramped back and got it."

The charge of the "Rough Riders" at the Battle of San Juan, July 1, 1898, became an American legend. Roosevelt reported to his commander that:

"You then sent me word to move forward in support of the regular cavalry, and I advanced the regiment in column of companies, each company deployed as skirmishers. We moved through several skirmish lines of the regiment ahead of us, as it seemed to me that our only chance was in rushing the entrenchments in front instead of firing at them from a distance.

"Accordingly we charged the blockhouse and entrenchments on the hill to our right against a heavy fire. It was taken in good style, the men of my regiment thus being the first to capture any fortified position and to break through the Spanish lines. The guidons of G and E troop were first at this point, but some of the men of A and B troops, who were with me personally, got in ahead of them. At the last wire fence up this hill I was obliged to abandon my horse, and after that we went on foot.

"After capturing this hill we first of all directed a heavy fire upon the San Juan hill to our left, which was at the time being assailed by the regular infantry and cavalry, supported by Captain Parker's Gatling guns. By the time San Juan was taken a large force had assembled on the hill we had previously captured, consisting not only of my own regiment, but of the Ninth and portions of the other cavalry regiments.

"We then charged forward under a very heavy fire across the valley against the Spanish entrenchments on the hill in the rear of San Juan hill. This we also took, capturing several prisoners.

"We then formed in whatever order we could and moved forward, driving the Spanish before us to the crest of the hills in front, which were immediately opposite the city of Santiago itself. Here I received orders to halt and hold the line on the hill's crest. I had at the time fragments of the Sixth Cavalry Regiment and an occasional infantryman under me – three or four hundred men all told. As I was the highest there I took command of all of them, and so continued till next morning.

''The Spaniards attempted to counter attack that afternoon, but were easily driven back, and then until after dark we remained under a heavy fire from their rifles and great guns, lying flat on our faces on a gentle slope just behind the crest.

''Captain parker's Gatling battery was run up to the right of my regiment and did most excellent and gallant service. In order to charge the men had of course been obliged to throw away their packs, and we had nothing to sleep in and nothing to eat. We were lucky enough, however, to find in the last blockhouse captured the Spanish dinners, still cooking, which we ate with relish. They consisted chiefly of rice and peas, with a big pot containing a stew of fresh meat, probably for the officers.

''We also distributed the captured Spanish blankets as far as they would go among our men, and gathered a good deal of Mauser ammunition for use in the Colt rapidfire guns, which were being brought up. That night we dug entrenchments across the front.''

Above: After the war, Roosevelt (seen here in ''Rough Riders'' uniform) became Governor of New York, and was maneuvered into the vice-presidency. On McKinley's death, Roosevelt became president, and in 1904 was elected in his own right.

Left: The Rough Riders played an important part in Roosevelt's career, as indicated by this cartoon of the president's visit to San Antonio, Texas, to participate in a Rough Rider reunion.

Above: The capture of Kettle Hill, just northeast of San Juan Hill but part of the same terrain feature, was captured by the Rough Riders and the 10th Cavalry Regiment, an African-American unit that was serving in the dismounted role with Sumner's division of dismounted cavalry.

Right: Lieutenant Colonel Theodore Roosevelt and some of his Rough Riders pose for the camera at the top of the hill.

Above: The battleship U.S.S. *Oregon* rounds Cape Horn on her storm-tossed passage from the Pacific Ocean to the Atlantic Ocean during the Spanish-American War. An up-to-date warship displacing 10,288 tons, the ship was armed with four 13-inch guns in two twin turrets, eight 8-inch guns in four twin turrets, four 6-inch guns, 20 6-pounder guns, and six 18-inch torpedo tubes. The time it took the ship to reach Sampson's squadron off Cuba was a major factor in the United States decision to press ahead with the construction of the Panama Canal.

Below: The battleship U.S.S. *Iowa*, as she appeared in her 1898 color scheme of tan and light gray. This single ship was based on an improved version of the design used for the "Indiana" class (U.S.S. *Indiana*, U.S.S. *Massachusetts*, and U.S.S. *Oregon*) with higher freeboard for better seaworthiness, as well as lightened armament of four 12-inch guns in two twin turrets, eight 8-inch guns in four twin turrets, six 4-inch guns, 20 6-pounder guns, and four 14-inch torpedo tubes. Like the "Indiana" class ships, the *Iowa* had reciprocating steam engines, but in this instance, the engines delivered 11,000 rather than 9,000 horsepower to two shafts for a maximum speed of 16 instead of 15 knots.

There was some fighting on July 2, mainly at long range, and both sides suffered considerable losses without any significant change in the overall situation.

Low morale

American morale was low after two days with little food and sleep. Shafter was now urged by some of his subordinate commanders to pull back to a stronger position on the Sevilla Heights, about five miles down the road from Santiago to Siboney. The V Corps commander telegraphed Washington that he was considering such a withdrawal, which would make it easier to supply the force and make it less prone to Spanish fire. Secretary of War Alger telegraphed back that "the effect on the country would be much better if V Corps stayed in its advance positions." Shafter therefore stayed put and demanded the surrender of Santiago. The demand was refused, but negotiations continued.

Meanwhile, Shafter urged the navy to break past the defenses of the entrance and move into Santiago Bay. But McKinley and the Navy Department were united in refusing to consider such a risky move. There was now every chance of a bitter

Admiral Dewey on his flagship during the Battle of Manila Bay.

dispute between the two services, which would almost certainly have become embarrassingly public, but the situation was saved by a Spanish move.

Acting under firm orders from Havana and Madrid to save his squadron if the loss of Santiago appeared imminent, Cervera tried to escape from Santiago on July 3. The Spanish admiral's plan was to reach the Spanish-held port of Cienfuegos, well to the northwest along Cuba's southern coast. The Spanish squadron of four armored cruisers and two torpedo boats, sailed with the flagship *Infanta Maria Teresa* leading the other cruisers, the *Vizcaya*, *Cristobal Colon*, and the *Almirante Oquendo*, followed by torpedo boats *Furo* and *Pluton*. The ships were all in poor mechanical condition, and while the cruisers were well armed, they were also very poorly protected.

Sampson was ashore meeting with Shafter, a fact that provides clear proof that the Americans were not expecting any such Spanish move, and Schley was in temporary command afloat. The sortie took Schley and the American squadron completely by surprise, but once the initial shock had passed, the Americans reacted with speed and vigor. The American force was considerably more powerful than the Spanish squadron and included, in addition to the two armed yachts *Vixen* and *Gloucester* that were maintaining an inshore watch, the armored cruiser *Brooklyn* (the flagship)

and the battleships *Texas, Iowa, Oregon,* and *Indiana.*

Suicide of the Spanish Squadron

The Spanish ships emerged from the mouth of Santiago Bay at 9:35 a.m. on July 3 and immediately headed west. The *Brooklyn* and *Texas* were right off the entrance to the bay, while the three

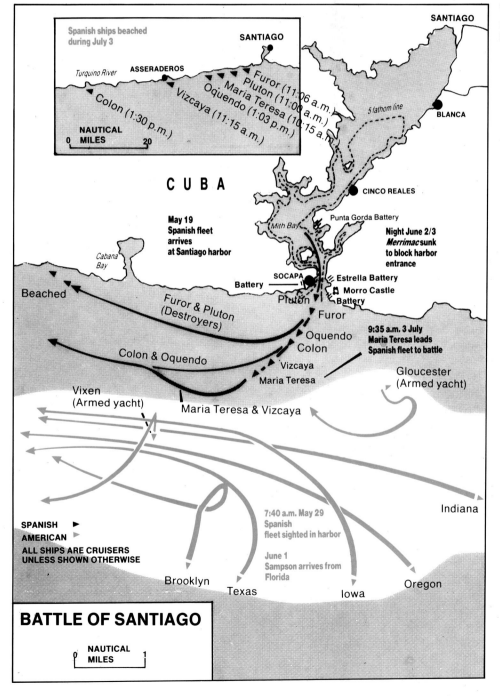

The U.S. victory in the naval Battle of Santiago.

BATTLE OF SANTIAGO

During the Battle of Santiago Bay, the *Cristobal Colon* comes under fire from the U.S.S. *Oregon* and U.S.S. *Iowa* (left).

other battleships were slightly to the east. Schley soon mustered his squadron for the pursuit, and the ships opened fire as soon as they were in range. The outcome was a foregone conclusion as the weight and accuracy of the American fire disabled the ships and forced them ashore. The first to go were the *Maria Teresa* and *Oquendo*, driven ashore west of Cabana Bay at 10:15 and 10:30 a.m. respectively. Next were the *Pluton* and *Furor*, which were beached slightly farther east at 11:00 and 11:06 a.m. respectively. The *Vizcaya* came ashore near Asseraderos at 11.15 a.m.; and the *Colon* was able to use her superior speed to avoid interception and move west until she was bracketed by 13-inch shells from the *Oregon* and forced ashore near the mouth of the Turquino River at 1:30 p.m. It was a stunning defeat; in a mere three hours and forty minutes after they opened fire at 9:50 a.m., the Americans destroyed all four cruisers and two torpedo boats, but suffered only two casualties (one sailor killed and another wounded), while 474 Spanish sailors were killed or wounded, and another 1,750 were taken prisoner.

On the same day, Colonel Federico Escario brought a reinforcement of 3,580 Spanish troops into Santiago along the Cobre Road without hindrance from the Cuban rebels whose job it was to stop them. With Spanish strength at nearly 17,140, command was exercised by General Jose Toral, who had replaced Linares after he had been wounded in the fighting on San Juan Heights. Demoralized by the defeat of Cervera's squadron, which convinced it that its isolation was complete, the Spanish garrison was also troubled by lack of ammunition and a shortage of food, while conditions for the citizens of Santiago were becoming bad because of a variety of shortages and deficiencies.

Negotiations for Surrender

Shafter continued to press the Spanish to surrender. The Spanish were not aware that conditions similar to their own, if not worse, were affecting the Americans. Shafter had received some reinforcements, allowing him to replace the Cuban rebels on his right flank with American soldiers, but his lack of artillery made it impossible to consider any assault on Santiago. About half of his men were

U.S. Casualties in the Spanish-American War

	ARMY	NAVY	MARINES	TOTAL
Number serving	280,564	22,875	3,321	306,760
Battle dead	369	10	6	385
Other deaths	2,061	None	None	2,061
Wounded	1,594	47	21	1,662

Washington D.C.
For further references
see pages
12, 47, 61, 67, 92

On July 14, 1899, General Toral surrendered Santiago to General Shafter and in effect ended the Spanish-American War.

already afflicted with dysentery, malaria, and typhoid. More worryingly, the first cases of the dreaded yellow fever had begun to appear among the forces besieging Santiago. Supplies were in very short supply, and Shafter was increasingly concerned that the imminent hurricane season could destroy his already tenuous line of supply and communication.

On July 10 and 11, Sampson contributed with a long-range naval bombardment, and on July 14 Toral agreed to surrender the whole of the Spanish IV Corps including more than 12,000 men in all the other garrisons of Santiago province. The agreement was formalized on July 15, and the Americans entered the city on July 17.

On July 11, General Miles had arrived off Santiago with a volunteer brigade. The task allotted to this force was an assault on the Spanish batteries west of Santiago Bay. Discovering that the surrender negotiations were well under way, Miles kept the brigade on board its ships un-

til the surrender had been implemented, and then sailed to Puerto Rico, a Spanish possession farther to the east.

The considerable achievement of V Corps at Santiago was marred by the revelation in the press about a major disagreement between Shafter and some of his senior subordinates. Worried by the spread of disease among the men, these officers had drafted a letter to Shafter proposing an immediate withdrawal from Cuba. The letter became known to the press before it reached Shafter, and thus Washington knew of the subordinates' fears and proposals ahead of the man to whom they were addressed. There was embarrassment on every side, but a useful side effect was the hastening of plans to evacuate the troops to an isolation camp which the Army Medical Department was creating at Montauk Point on Long Island for the treatment of those with tropical diseases. Another important consequence of the army's Cuban campaign, and its experience of the effects of disease and climate, was

Corporal, 13th Cavalry Regiment, U.S. Army, Mexican Expedition, 1916.

The 1912 pattern olive-drab service uniform was made both in wool for winter use and cotton for summer wear, and the cavalry equipment of the same year's pattern included a cartridge belt and bandolier. From 1907, mounted men were issued with russet-strap leather leggings. Weapons were the M1903 Springfield rifle and the M1911 Colt semi-automatic pistol.

the Army Medical Department's long-term research program to find the cause of yellow fever.

Early in August 1898, V Corps had to be withdrawn because of the spread of yellow fever, and it was replaced by a number of "immune regiments" thought – erroneously - to be immune to the disease. It is a telling statistic of the Cuban campaign that while only 379 Americans were killed in battle, more than 5,000 died of disease.

A Tricky Situation in the Philippines

Meanwhile, in the Philippines, Dewey was continuing to walk a difficult tightrope. Throughout May and June, the American naval commander waited for the arrival of the ground forces he had requested. At the same time, he kept in constant touch with Aguinaldo, leader of the Filipino rebels occupying the area around Manila

American soldiers on board the S.S. *Rio de Janeiro* as she departs from the West Coast, headed for the Philippines.

PHÉNOL SODIQUE

STOPS BLEEDING   HEALS ALL WOUNDS

There was little that could not be exploited by advertising men, as indicated by this "scene" from the U.S.S. *Olympia* during the Battle of Manila Bay.

Elwell Otis
For further references
see pages
58, 59, 64, 65, 66, 67

who were keeping General Jaudene's 13,000-man garrison bottled up in the city. The Americans and the Filipino rebels shared a common cause, namely the defeat of the Spanish, but relations between the two allies deteriorated steadily over the weeks, mainly because of a difference in longer-term objectives. The Filipinos who already controlled most parts of the Philippine archipelago except the areas immediately around the larger towns, wanted complete independence. The tide of public and political opinion in the United States was swaying against this view, and the president himself favored American possession of the Philippines. Aguinaldo sought to strengthen the Filipino position for independence by establishing an interim government with himself as president. On August 6, this government asked foreign

governments to recognize the independence of the Philippines.

The army had meanwhile completed its preparations to support Dewey in the Philippines. Sailing from San Francisco and other west coast ports, Major General Wesley Merritt's VIII Corps reached the islands by July 30 with a strength that eventually reached 2,000 regular soldiers (mainly the 14th and 23rd Infantry Regiments) and 13,000 volunteers. Major General Elwell Otis's second wave arrived early in August. The troops had loaded their equipment and themselves without confusion, and they disembarked at Cavite in the same effective fashion. Despite the long sea crossing, the men were enthusiastic and fit, and could therefore move without delay toward Manila.

By early August, Merritt had about

8,500 of his men in position south of Manila, immediately behind the lines occupied by part of the 10,000-man rebel force investing the city. Aguinaldo had long been ready to attack, and Dewey could have provided him with gunfire support from ships cruising close in-shore, but Dewey had delayed until American land forces were ready. The Spanish governor was already prepared to surrender, but wanted to hand the city and his forces over to the Americans rather than the Filipinos. The situation was further complicated by the insistence of the Spanish government in far-off Madrid that there would be no surrender until the garrison had made at least a token show of resistance.

Dewey and Merritt finally persuaded the Filipinos into a compromise: the Americans of Brigadier General Anderson's 2nd Infantry Division would be allowed to pass through the rebel lines when the ''fighting'' began south of the city. Aguinaldo agreed to the compromise with great reluctance, for he had been asked to pull his forces back as the American units passed through them.

The Battle of Manila

On the morning of August 13, Dewey's ships launched a short bombardment against the Spanish defenses, and the 2nd Infantry Division started to move through the rebel positions in two columns centered on the brigades of Brigadier Generals Greene on the left and Arthur MacArthur on the right. At the best of times such a maneuver is difficult; as this instance involved poorly trained

The ceremony marking the transfer of power in Cuba to the American interim administration on January 1, 1899, at Pinar del Rio.

55

Transfer of power to the Americans in the Philippines did not proceed as smoothly as it had in Cuba, and American ownership of the islands resulted in the Philippine Insurrection. This uprising soon became a major and long-festering guerrilla campaign marked by episodes such as this wrecking of a train on the Bamban Bridge in Luzon during 1900.

units, it is hardly surprising that American and rebel units became mixed. It is no more surprising that some of the rebel units then began to fire on the Spanish positions just to their north. Such an episode could have threatened the Spanish intention to offer only token resistance, and American officers moved quickly to end the firing. The Spanish surrendered as the Americans advanced into Manila, and American losses in the Manila campaign were therefore restricted to 17 dead and 105 wounded.

The formal surrender was signed on the following day. Dewey had cut the telegraph cable to the islands when he first entered Manila Bay, and both sides were unaware of the fact that, two days earlier, the Madrid government had signed a protocol ending hostilities.

The Capture of Puerto Rico

The last episode of the Spanish-American War was the occupation of Puerto Rico. Miles had sailed with 5,000 men after the surrender of Santiago, intending to land at Punta Fajardo on the eastern end of the island where there was a small Spanish garrison. He would then advance on San Juan, the capital, where the bulk of the island's 7,000 defenders were grouped.

But after leaving Cuba, Miles changed his plan. The general wanted to avoid a combined army/navy assault of the kind that had caused problems in the Cuban campaign; he also wanted to secure tactical surprise. The new landing site was Guanica, an ungarrisoned spot toward the western end of the island's south coast, where an unopposed landing was made on July 25. Miles had already called for reinforcements, and on August 4 units of Major General Brooke's I Corps landed at Guanica and at two points farther west. The whole campaign was a minor masterpiece of planning and execution, and the American forces advanced north against minimal opposition. The news of the war's end arrived in time to halt operations on August 12, before Miles's 15,200-man force was faced with the main Spanish strength outside San Juan.

Negotiations between the United States and Spain continued through the fall of 1898 in Paris, the capital of France, and the Spanish-American War was brought to a formal end by the Treaty of Paris, signed on December 10, 1898. Under the terms of the treaty,

Spain renounced all claims to sovereignty over Cuba, which became an independent country, ceded Puerto Rico and the Pacific island of Guam to the United States, and sold the Philippines to the United States for $20,000,000. The Spanish-American War was dubbed "the splendid little war," and did indeed catapult the United States onto the world stage. It also highlighted many organizational and technical deficiencies, especially in the army; moreover, it was very expensive. It is interesting to note that, of the 275,000 men mobilized as a result of public pressure, perhaps only 20,000 fired a shot. Even so, as late as 1959 some 100,000 men, together with an equal number of dependents, were receiving war pensions totaling about $150,000,000 per year.

While its fortunes were developing in overseas campaigns, the United States was still developing its large system of coastal fortifications. Emplaced in these defenses were weapons such as this 270-mm (10·63-inch) mortar of 1885, really a heavy howitzer designed to lob high explosive shells high into the air so that they would plunge down onto their targets.

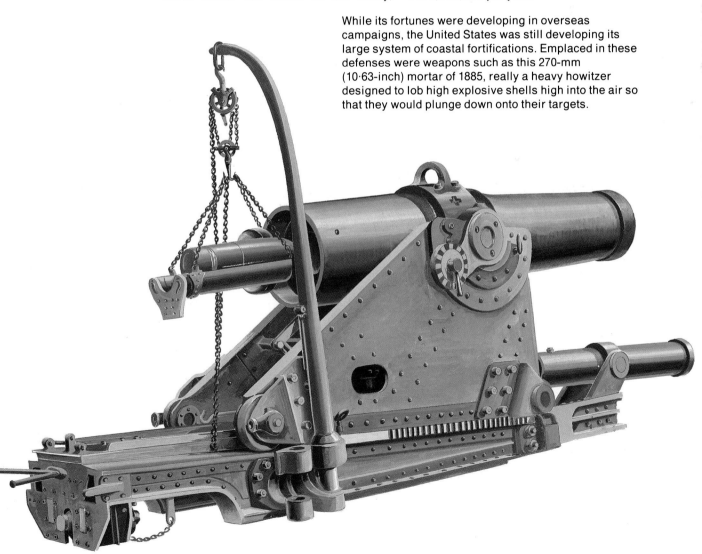

A scene typical of the Philippine Insurrection, this 1899 photograph shows American soldiers manhandling a 47-mm Hotchkiss gun over a bridge that had been temporarily repaired after its destruction by the guerrillas.

From Bad to Worse in the Philippines

After the surrender of the Spanish there was only a brief respite in Philippine operations, but relations between the Americans and Filipinos continued to deteriorate. This process was accelerated in December 1898 after news had been received of the United States' purchase of the islands.

After the capture of Manila, Aguinaldo had established a provisional republic with its capital at Malolos, northwest of Manila. Here a congress began the task of preparing a republican constitution. In January 1899, the United States formally declared its ownership of the Philippines and its plan to extend American political control over all the islands of the archipelago. In response, the Filipino congress ratified its constitution to establish a Filipino state and prepared to resist the Americans.

On February 4, 1899, the day before Congress was due to ratify the Treaty of Paris, an American soldier fired on and killed a Filipino soldier, and the Philippine Insurrection began. The circumstances of this spark are still obscure, but it is probable that either a Filipino patrol deliberately challenged an American guard post in the hope of causing an incident that could be used for Filipino propaganda, or simply that the volatility of the situation got out of hand.

The Philippine Insurrection

Under the command of Otis, VIII Corps responded quickly and effectively. Otis had a nominal strength of 21,000 against an estimated 40,000 Filipinos under Aguinaldo's military commander, General Luna. But only 12,000 of these American troops could be committed, as the other 9,000 were volunteers scheduled to return to the United States. Even so, their superior training and weapons allowed the Americans to take the offensive over the next two days. It was a conventional infantry battle, in which the Americans had the advantages of naval gunfire support. For the loss of 337 of their own men (59 killed and 278 wounded), the Americans drove the Filipinos from Manila with the loss of between 2,000 and 5,000 dead.

The Filipino forces fled to the north. Some American military and political leaders believed that their flight signaled the approaching end of hostilities, but this was in fact very far from being the case. The campaign rapidly spread throughout the island of Luzon and then stretched out south to the islands around the Visayan Sea. Aguinaldo had already planned an urban uprising within Manila, but Otis suspected that something was in the offing, and prompt action in the city soon ended all hope of any rebel success in the heart of the growing American power structure.

The Americans responded to the

American success in the Philippine Insurrection depended on soldiers such as these, seen here just before their departure on a scouting mission. The guerrillas had no formal structure that could be engaged and defeated by conventional military measures, so the war was decided by small-scale operations in which guerrillas were killed or captured, while, at the same time, the support that the remaining guerrillas enjoyed was removed.

It was only in the early stages of the Philippine Insurrection that American artillery could find worthwhile targets with any regularity.

spread of the insurrection by sending out task forces to find, fix, and destroy: they found very little, and fixed virtually nothing, but did manage to destroy many Filipino villages. This senseless tactic had no effect other than to strengthen Filipino resolve and to provide copy for American journalists whose increasingly despondent reports soon began to reveal the truth about events in the Philippines to the general public.

The real nature of the Philippine problem was neatly encapsulated by a Mr. Bass of Harper's Weekly: "...various expeditions have taken place, principally in the island of Luzon. These expeditions resulted in our taking from the insurgent government certain territory. Some of this territory we have occupied; the rest we have returned to the insurgents in more or less mutilated condition, depending on whether the policy of the hour was to carry on a bitter war against a barbarous enemy, or to bring enlightenment to an ignorant people, deceived as to our motives." Bass then concluded that the outlook was "blacker now than it has been since the beginning of the war" for several reasons, including the fact that "the whole population of the islands sympathizes with the insurgents; only those natives whose immediate self-interest requires it are friendly to us."

Wrong Tactics

The Americans also hoped to put down the rebellion with capture of Malolos, which was taken by MacArthur's brigade at the cost of 550 casualties. But one place was as good as another to a revolutionary government such as that headed by Aguinaldo, and nothing concrete was achieved by MacArthur's operation. There was no vital administrative center to capture, and the beaten insurgent army dissolved, flowed north, and then reassembled once it was beyond the immediate reach of the Americans.

By late spring, it was clear that the Americans were going to have a hard time crushing the insurrection. The problem was appreciated firsthand in the Philippines by Otis and his increasingly despondent men, and also in Washington

by McKinley's administration. It was clear that the first requirement was additional troops in the islands, and the War Department acted with commendable speed: it ordered the immediate despatch to the islands of more regular troops and set about raising ten additional volunteer regiments. By the late summer of 1899, VIII Corps had been swelled by an extra 35,000 men, and more men were on their way. More than 100,000 men served in the Philippines before the insurrection was ended.

Guerrilla Warfare

The Filipinos were short of all military supplies including small arms and ammunition. After a few early encounters, the insurgents avoided open clashes, relying instead on the tactics of guerrilla warfare. Thus the war became one of ambushes and surprise attacks, where the Filipino bolo (a short sword with a blade

Although the Krag-Jorgensen bolt-action magazine-fed rifle had been adopted in 1892, most American infantry in the Spanish-American War and resulting Philippine Insurrection still used the single-shot Springfield Model 1889 rifle firing a black-powder round. Soldiers were rarely grouped as closely as this during the fighting.

This illustration of the Battle of Quingua, fought on April 23, 1899, highlights one of the few pitched battles of the Philippine Insurrection before the campaign descended to the level of guerrilla warfare.

BATTLE OF PACEO, MANILA, FEB 4 & 5 1899, AM. LOSS KILLED 22, W'945, PHILIPS OVER 1000.

The Battle of Paco, on the outskirts of Manila, was another battle of the Philippine Insurrection's early phase. Fought on February 14, 1899, the fight cost the Filipinos more than 1,000 casualties, while the Americans suffered 22 killed and 145 wounded.

Henry L. Lawton
For further references
see pages
34, 35, 36, 38, 43, 65, 66

between 12 and 18 inches long) and other traditional weapons proved very effective. Such warfare also allowed the Filipinos to exploit their knowledge of the jungle and mountain terrain where most of the fighting took place.

Despite their large overall strength, the American soldiers found that the nature of the enemy and the terrain, which had few roads and was generally very difficult, forced them to revert to the type of fighting familiar from the Indian wars. Once again, therefore, field forces of small size became standard, and the rifle and bayonet were once more the fighting man's main weapons.

The Americans also discovered to their cost that the Filipinos did not abide by any conventional ''rules of war.'' Prisoners were tortured and killed; ambushes were launched under cover of a flag of truce; and rebels approached unsuspecting American troops wearing captured uniforms. Unfortunately, the Americans responded at times by lowering their own standards, which did much

to alienate the Filipinos even more.

VIII Corps nevertheless kept the Filipinos under constant pressure, using its overall strength and better organization to keep the rebels, already badly organized and lacking coordination, off balance and on the defensive. Slowly, the Americans began to extend their control over Luzon and the other important islands.

From April 1899, the men of VIII Corps undertook a series of carefully coordinated offensives designed to give them control of Luzon's main lines of communication and population centers, which was essential in restoring stability of administration and normalizing the economic life of the islands. Steps had already been taken with the initial sweep in February that had captured Malolos and secured the lines of the Pasig River, which cut the main line of communication between Filipino forces in the northern and southern halves of Luzon.

General Lawton, comparatively new to the Philippines after his part in the Santiago campaign, was despatched by Otis during April to strike south toward Santa Cruz in the region of Laguna de Bay. At the same time, MacArthur, now a major general, was launched north from Malolos through the central plain toward San Fernando. By May, both drives had achieved considerable success, and the extension of American power south and north from the Manila area made it increasingly difficult for the Filipinos to continue a properly organized resistance. Aguinaldo was forced to flee north, where he found refuge in the mountains.

With the arrival of the rainy season in the early summer of 1899, the Americans called a halt to further offensive operations, which would in any case need more manpower. Operations up to this time had led to 1,026 engagements, resulting in American casualties of 245 killed, 490 wounded, and 118 captured. Claimed Filipino losses were 3,854 killed, 1,193 wounded, and 6,572 captured.

Additional men, boosting American strength to 45,000 men, arrived in the fall, when better weather allowed operations against the rebels to be resumed .

Three-pronged offensive

In September 1899, Otis launched a three-pronged offensive by division-sized forces into northern Luzon against the main part of the Filipinos' surviving strength. On the left, Brigadier General Loyd Wheaton's force sailed from Manila to San Fabian, landed, and moved inland to defeat a rebel force at San Jacinto and link up with the central American drive at Dagupan. In the center, MacArthur advanced through Tarlac to reach Dagupan. And on the right, Lawton recaptured San Isidro and advanced toward San Fabian on Lingayen Gulf, despite appalling conditions – so bad that the column averaged only 20 miles a week for six weeks.

Colonel Young, commanding the cavalry element of Lawton's division,

The ammunition train and reserves of Colonel Frederick Funston's 20th Kansas Volunteers move through Caloocan after the regiment's main strength had driven the guerrillas out of the town.

Some of the peoples who gave the Americans their greatest problems in the Philippines were the Moros of Mindanao Island. It seems indicative that this 1900 photograph contains relatively few men of fighting age.

finally received permission to break away from the slower infantry and decided to speed his advance by living off the land after abandoning his supporting wagons. Young's troopers surprised Aguinaldo's Rear guard near San Pedro and captured the Filipino leader's mother and son. Yet again, however, Aguinaldo and most of his guerrillas escaped.

By this time, the war had lost all resemblance to an orthodox campaign, yet Otis was now so convinced he was winning that he continued to press ahead with his effort to extend central control from Manila. With a strength of more than 60,000 men, Otis created a fan of outposts around the capital, which tied down a large proportion of his effective strength. During December, the commander in the Philippines was so sure that he was winning that he telegraphed Washington four times to inform the authorities that the war was over.

Some of Otis's subordinate commanders were not so sure. Lawton described the Filipino rebels as "the bravest men I have ever seen." MacArthur was not as fulsome, but still nearer the mark with his comment that "...wherever throughout the archipelago there is a group of the insurgent army, it is a fact beyond dispute that all the contiguous towns contribute to the maintenance thereof...Intimidation has undoubtedly accomplished much to this end; but fear as the only motive is hardly sufficient to account for the united and apparently spontaneous action of several millions of people."

Undeterred, Otis continued with his program of fanning outposts out from Manila and sending punitive expeditions to other islands. Yet local resistance increased, and the Americans' steadily lengthening lines of communication became irresistible – and vulnerable – targets for the rebels. Trails and paths were blocked or "mined" with drop traps, the rebels ambushed supply parties and outpost garrisons, and local villagers stole small arms and ammunition.

The policy adopted by Otis was therefore not very effective in terms of its success rate and practical use of manpower. Yet it did provide a measure of success, and during the winter of 1899-1900, continued American operations did succeed in eliminating most of the last rebel elements from the region around Manila and securing the vital lines of communication in central Luzon.

Otis Replaced by MacArthur

By March 1900, the army had extended its grip to southern Luzon and the Visayan Islands; and in May, Otis was confident that the insurrection was beaten and asked to be relieved. As 1900 was a Congressional election year, McKinley was concerned that Republican chances were being affected by the slow pace of Otis's program, and he readily agreed to the request. The new commander was MacArthur, and, contrary to Otis's belief, the insurrection was not over. The Filipino rebels were certainly weaker than they had been, but they were still full of fight.

MacArthur had 70,000 men at his disposal and decided to follow the same basic tactics as Otis while adding some new elements of his own. Initially, they were a resounding failure. MacArthur launched an amnesty plan, but only 5,000 Filipinos came in to swear allegiance to the American flag; he offered 30 pesos for every rifle surrendered, but only 140 weapons were turned in. While punitive expeditions were still sent to other islands, isolated from each other by gunboat blockade, MacArthur offered their chiefs bribes to halt the fighting; he spent a considerable sum only to find that the chiefs did nothing.

MacArthur now wanted to try harsher tactics, but could not secure authorization from Washington at a time when the administration was more concerned with placating the voters. Imperialism was a major issue in the elections that year; and Aguinaldo, seeing that a Democratic majority in Congress was his only hope, urged the rebels to greater efforts so that the Philippines issue would remain in the headlines, and therefore in the minds of the voters. The Republican victory was

U.S. Army Campaign Streamers of the Philippine Insurrection

Manila	February 4 – March 17, 1899
Illoilo	February 8-12, 1899
Malolos	March 24 – August 16, 1899
Laguna de Bay	April 8-17, 1899
San Isidro	April 21 – May 30, 1899
	October 15 – November 19, 1899
Zapote River	June 13, 1899
Cavite	October 7-13, 1899
	January 4 – February 9, 1899
Tarlac	November 5-20, 1899
San Fabian	November 6-19, 1899
Mindanao	July 4, 1902 – December 31, 1904
Jolo	May 1-24, 1905
	June 11-15, 1913

therefore a major blow to Aguinaldo.

With the elections out of the way, the administration gave MacArthur a freer hand and considerable reinforcements. At the end of 1901, MacArthur placed the islands under martial law, and mass arrests and internment followed. At this point, the rebel movement faltered for the first time, and the pro-American Federal Party began to grow in strength. Over the previous few months, a number of morally and physically exhausted rebels had come over to the American side, and American commanders had been able to use Filipinos as irregular scouts.

The Philippine Scouts: a Decisive Weapon

In February 1901, MacArthur received Congressional permission to raise ''a body of native troops, not exceeding 12,000, called 'Scouts','' initially made up of between 30 and 50 companies of 100 men each under the command of American officers. This marked a major turning point in the war, for the Philippine Scouts proved very loyal and at last gave the Americans access to local knowledge that had previously been the preserve of the rebels.

The Philippine Scouts played a significant part in the first real break won by the Americans in the insurrection, the capture of Aguinaldo. The event resulted from the capture, by troops under Brigadier General Frederick Funston, of a rebel courier. This man was carrying, among other messages, an order from Aguinaldo to a chief ordering the latter to send 400 fighting men as soon as possible. The courier also revealed that Aguinaldo was in Isabela, the mountainous northeastern province of Luzon.

A resourceful volunteer officer, Funston rapidly planned and with some difficulty secured official permission for an effort to take the Filipino leader. Funston instructed 81 Maccabebe tribesmen of the Philippine Scouts to masquerade as the men ordered by Aguinaldo, and with Funston himself and four other officers acting the part of prisoners, this party moved 100 miles through rebel territory to reach Aguinaldo's headquarters. Funston's party took Aguinaldo prisoner and then returned to American-held territory. It was a quite extraordinary achievement. Aguinaldo later swore allegiance to the American flag and then issued a surrender proclamation.

Taft Arrives as Governor

Another important break for the Americans was the July 1901 appoint-

The French 5-mm M 1897 gun introduced the quick firing concept. The Nordenfeldt breech screw is well shown here, as is the box trail construction which restricted the gun's elevation. This was the first truly modern artillery used by the U.S.

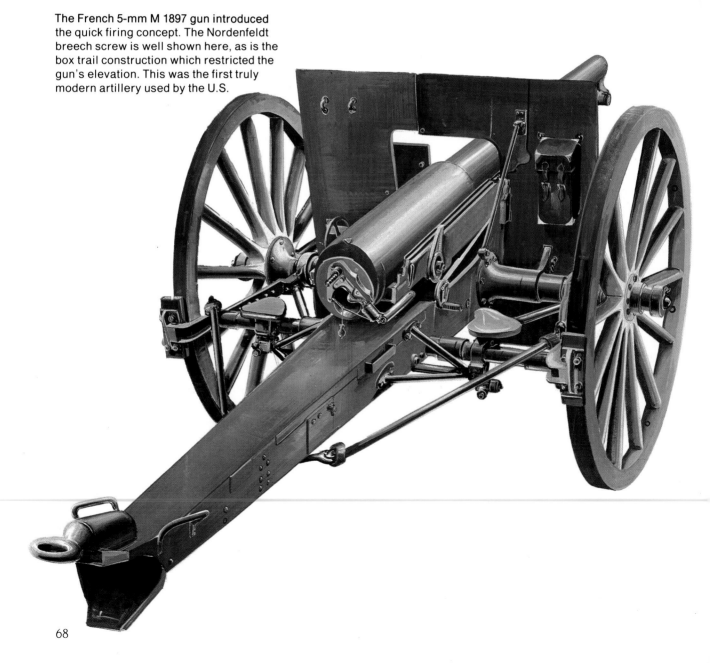

The far-sighted, impartial, and fair administration of William Taft in the Philippines was a major factor in the eventual success of the United States in the islands. The experience helped Taft's career considerably; it culminated in his election as President in 1908.

ment of William Howard Taft (later the 27th president) as civilian governor of the islands. At the same time, MacArthur was replaced as military commander by Major General Adna R. Chaffee, who was placed firmly under the overall control of Taft. To make sure that the military did in fact follow the governor's orders, control of all military funds, including pay, was entrusted to Taft.

Taft saw his major task as being the establishment of an effective American administration in the islands. As the governor's policy began to produce results, support for the rebel cause declined. The effect of this American policy was thus considerable, and it has been graphically said that "rebel operations now began to resemble writhing ganglia of a headless body." With their position worsening almost by the day, the rebels became desperate and turned more frequently to atrocities.

Unfortunately for the American cause, these incidents resulted in a number of very harsh measures by some army commanders, most notably Brigadier Generals Bell and "Roaring Jake" Smith. Early in 1902, Bell captured Malvar, one of the most important rebel leaders still at

large on one of the Visayan Islands, where the people were still firmly on the side of the rebels. "To combat such a population," Bell later said, "it is necessary to make the state of war as insupportable as possible...by keeping the minds of the people in such a state of anxiety and apprehension that living under such conditions will soon become unbearable. Let acts, not words, convey the intention." What Bell and other such officers practiced, however, was the type of counterinsurgency warfare fought by Weyler in Cuba, where such tactics had led the press to dub the Spanish commander "Butcher" and call for American intervention.

Fortunately for the American cause, however, Taft was firmly against such operations. Taft insisted that a Marine Corps officer, Major L. W. T. Waller, should be court-martialed for executing treacherous native guides. This court martial revealed the tactics of Waller's superior, Smith, who had told Waller: "I want no prisoners, I want you to burn and kill; the more you burn and kill, the better it will please me." Smith was also court-martialed.

Far-sighted Civil Administration

Taft acted quickly against all such practices and concentrated on winning the hearts of the Filipinos. For $7,000,000, the Americans bought from the Vatican 410,000 acres of land that were sold in parcels to peasants on easy terms. A vast civil affairs program was put in hand, and a major educational effort was started with an initial call for 1,000 American teachers.

Taft placed great emphasis on a return to civilian-controlled normality, with an increasing emphasis on the importance of the Philippine Constabulary instead of the army for the elimination of what were now ladrones (outlaw robbers), not rebels. Even so, many months passed before a large number of small engagements whittled down the last elements of armed resistance. Early in 1902, unrest among the Moslem Moro tribesmen of Mindanao and the islands of the Sulu archipelago (particularly Jolo) flared; it had not been

William Taft
For further references
see pages
79, 90, 122

A realization of the value of propaganda to support military ventures is shown by the posing of this photograph of the Philippine Insurrection and by the original caption, which reads "How United States Soldiers Were Met by Conquered Natives."

John J. Pershing
For further references see pages 126, 127, 130

fully eliminated by the time President Theodore Roosevelt announced the formal end of the Philippine Insurrection on July 4, 1902. The army's experience in the insurrection made operations against these Moslem rebels easier, and by 1905 the most troublesome of the rebel bands had been eliminated after a small but exhausting campaign led by officers such as Colonel John W. Duncan, Captain John J. Pershing, and Captain Frank R. McCoy. Even so, sporadic revolts continued throughout the country up to 1916, as it took time for the benefits of improved conditions to filter out from the cities to major towns, small towns, villages, and finally the countryside.

Some 4,243 American soldiers died in the suppression of the Philippine Insurrection, and many thousands more were to die in the following years from the effects of tropical disease; 2,818

Americans were also wounded. It is estimated that the rebels lost between 16,000 and 20,000 dead, and that civilian deaths totaled about 200,000, including 100,000 who died of starvation in the famines caused by the war.

Eyes on China

With American imperialist ambitions already on the increase, the acquisition of the Philippines, lying off the coast of China, sparked an upsurge of American interest in the Manchu empire. The Philippines were seen as an asset in themselves, but just as important, as an ideal base for American economic and humanitarian efforts in China. At the end of the 19th century, China was a dying empire whose internal squabbles and weakness were an open invitation to

The Boxers
For further references
see pages
74, 76, *77*, 78, 79

those with territorial and economic ambitions on the Asiatic mainland. The overall weakness of China was fully revealed in the Sino-Japanese War, which began in 1894 over rivalry for predominance in Korea. The war resulted in a clear-cut victory for Japan, which thus entered the lists as a world power. The Japanese victory was followed in April 1895 by the Treaty of Shimonoseki, which resulted in Chinese recognition of Korean independence, a huge Chinese indemnity to Japan, and Japanese possession of Formosa, the Pescadores Islands, and the Liaotung peninsula, though the latter had to be given up after pressure from Russia, France, and Germany.

Faced with Japanese rivalry for commercial and political dominance in China, the European powers scrambled to win similar concessions from China between 1895 and 1900. The great threat was a partition of China, though this was steadily opposed by the United States and the United Kingdom. In September 1899, the United States was able to announce that it had secured the agreement of all interested countries for the continued existence of an "open door" policy in China.

The Boxer Rebellion

This foreign intervention raised the anger of the already isolationist Chinese, and a group of young fanatics created an organization known as the Society of the Righteous Harmonious Fists, or Boxers as they were called in the West. Committed to keeping China completely Chinese and enjoying the tacit but influential support of the Dowager Empress Tzu Hsi, the Boxers started to fight foreign influence in China. By 1900, the actions of the Boxers had brought much of northeastern China to the verge of rebellion. In the northern provinces, the Boxers concentrated on Christian missionaries and their converts, many hundreds of whom were killed.

The foreign powers protested strongly, which achieved nothing but a further es-

A major component of the U.S. Army's China Relief Expedition of 1900 was the 9th Infantry Regiment. This photograph shows soldiers of the regiment on a vessel being towed to Tientsin by steam tug.

The U.S.S. *Monocacy* with a hole in her port side as a result of a Chinese shell hit is seen here against the backdrop of the burning city of Tongu.

calation of the violence. Increasingly concerned about the deterioration of events in China, the foreign powers began to foresee the need for military intervention, and from June 1900, warships assembled off Tientsin, the port nearest Peking. From this fleet, a force of 485 men from several nations was sent to guard the legations in Peking.

As the situation worsened in Chih-li and Shantung provinces, an allied force of 2,000 men, including 112 Americans, landed in Tientsin on June 10 under the command of a British officer, Admiral E. H. Seymour, to move to Peking. This first relief expedition was a complete failure, for it was halted by a much superior Chinese force at Tang Ts'u and forced to

turn back. The expedition suffered 300 casualties before it returned to the allied fleet on June 26.

Bombardment of the Ta-Ku Forts

While the first expedition was suffering its reverse, more successful matters were occurring in its rear. Tientsin lies on the Hai River some distance from the open sea, and the allies were concerned that navigation up the river to the port could be stopped by the Chinese forts at Ta-Ku at the river mouth. An ultimatum was issued for these forts to surrender, and when the forts replied by opening fire on the allied fleet, the ships returned fire, and on June 17, landing parties stormed and captured the forts. Involved in this episode were ships of the U.S. Navy's China Squadron, commanded by Rear Admiral Louis Kempff.

In Peking, the news of the loss of the Ta-Ku forts resulted in widespread rioting on June 20, culminating in the murder of the German ambassador, Baron Klemens von Kettler, and the siege of the western legations. It had already become clear that a general uprising against foreigners and their influence was imminent, and the numbers of people in the legations had been swollen by the arrival of hundreds of other foreigners and Chinese converts to Christianity. The legation compound, held by about 600 soldiers and armed civilians, now faced a siege by a very much larger number of Boxers supported by imperial troops.

McKinley's administration was unwilling to become involved, especially during an election year, when the Democratic opposition might use the opportunity to

embarrass the Republicans with the implications of any international incident. But the United States was already involved, and McKinley agreed that American forces would have to participate in the multi-national effort to relieve those under siege in the legation area of Peking. Even so, McKinley was at great pains to limit American involvement with the intervening powers, and Secretary of State John Hay therefore told the American ambassador in China that "...we have no policy in China except to protect with energy American interests and especially American citizens...There must be no alliances." To reinforce this fact with the interventionist powers, Hay circulated a second "open door" note on July 3, reasserting that it was American policy "to seek a solution which may bring about permanent safety and peace to China, preserve Chinese territorial and administrative entity, protect all rights guaranteed to friendly powers by treaty and international law, and safeguard for

The multinational nature of the allied response to the Boxer Rebellion is evident in this Japanese illustration of the attack on Tientsin which, naturally enough, emphasizes the Japanese contribution. (Picture taken from an old book in the Library of Congress).

the world the principle of equal and impartial trade with all parts of the Chinese Empire."

A Major Relieving Force

After the first relief expedition had been stopped, the allied powers had taken steps to despatch a considerably larger force to Tientsin, from which a second relief expedition could advance to Peking. As a result of the Philippine Insurrection, the U.S Army already had sizeable forces in the area and could therefore contribute one of the larger elements of this second expedition. MacArthur was unhappy to weaken his forces in the Philippines when every man was needed to fight Aguinaldo's forces, but recognized the need for American support of the international effort against the Boxers. He therefore agreed to the immediate departure of the 9th Infantry Regiment, to be followed rapidly by the 14th Infantry Regiment and some artillery. Other units, including the 6th Cavalry Regiment, came from the United States. Manila became the rear base for these forces, with Nagasaki in Japan as the advance base. The American contingent, officially designated the China Relief Expedition and commanded by General Chaffee, eventually totaled 2,500 men, including a battalion of Marines.

The first task of this relief expedition was to capture Tientsin as a secure base of operations, which was accomplished on July 13. An American contingent was heavily involved in the 5,000-man allied force, which stormed the city walls and then captured the fort. The 9th Infantry Regiment suffered notably heavy losses, including its commander, Colonel E. H. Liscum.

In addition to 2,500 Americans, by August 4, the relief expedition included 4,800 Russian, 3,000 British, and 800 French troops. The later arrival of other detachments from Austria-Hungary, Germany, Italy, and Japan raised strength to 18,700 men, but the expedition was unusual in its lack of an overall commander. The allies had decided to work on a cooperative basis.

The second relief expedition set off from Tientsin toward Peking on August 4, and followed the 70-mile line of the river with its parallel railroad. The Chinese put a force of 10,000 men into the field to block the expedition's advance, but it was decisively beaten at Yang T'sun on August 5/6. At Yang T'sun, the French were detached to guard the allied line of communication as the rest of the expedi-

This American photograph shows another part of the allied effort against the Boxers: a piece of British field artillery.

tion pressed ahead. Resistance was now only sporadic, and the expedition arrived outside the walls of Peking on August 12.

The Capture of Peking

The allied plan was an immediate assault to break through the Tung Pien Gate and get into the Outer City. The limitations of cooperative command soon became evident, for the Russians broke through too quickly on August 13, were then driven back and lost cohesion, and had to be rescued by other parts of the allied force. A more carefully coordinated plan was put together for August 14. The Japanese were repulsed as they tried to storm the Ch'i Hua Gate, but the allies were more successful in other sectors.

The main American strength supported the Russians in a successful drive through the Tung Pien Gate. Two companies of the 14th Infantry Regiment assaulted the northeast section of the Tartar Wall and pushed back the defenders. First to reach the top of the wall was Bugler Calvin P. Titus, who raised the American flag. From this position, the Americans were well sited to support the men of the British contingent, who waded under the main defenses at the Water Gate and advanced into the Outer City. The allied force now drove through to relieve the legations, where the defenders had by now been driven back to the British compound.

In the legations, the small military and civilian force had held back almost incessant Chinese attacks for eight weeks. The guard detachments had lost four officers and 49 men killed, together with nine officers and 136 men wounded, while the civilian contingent had lost 12 killed and 23 wounded.

The allied expedition also relieved the P'ei Tang cathedral compound, where 40

American artillery in action during the allied advance on Peking in 1900.

French and Italian marines, some priests and nuns, and 3,000 of their converts had held back nonstop Boxer attacks, in the process suffering the deaths of seven marines, four priests, and 300 Chinese Christians.

On August 15, Light Battery F of the 5th U.S. Artillery Regiment, commanded by Captain Henry J. Reilly, blasted the Ch'i Hua Gate leading to the Inner City after First Lieutenant Charles P. Summerall had coolly walked out under heavy fire to chalk an aiming spot for the gunners on the gate timbers. A few salvoes opened the way for the allied troops to occupy the center of Peking. The American contingent played no part in this occupation or subsequent allied operations. Casualties in the China Relief Expedition had been only slightly more than 200, but McKinley

This illustration shows a combined American, Japanese and British assault on one of Peking's gates during the relief of the legations held under siege. (Taken from an old book in the Library of Congress).

Below Right: The Boxers were completely outclassed in weapons by the allies, but had larger numbers and fought with fanatical determination. This illustration shows Boxers trying to halt the advance of an American column.

was now anxious to avoid further involvement as the other allies set about mopping up the last elements of Boxer resistance, and the main strength of the American force was pulled back to the Philippines before the onset of winter.

Allied troops moved into the Imperial City on August 28, and between September 1900 and May 1901, a series of sweeps against the Boxer remnants took

place. A number of them were made by German forces under the command of the overenthusiastic Field Marshal Alfred von Waldersee. The dowager empress had already fled to a secure spot in Shensi province, and after the Russians had occupied Manchuria between September 4 and October 10, she finally agreed to allied demands on December 26.

During the long period of negotiation that followed, the Americans contributed a small regular army force to the allied strength that remained in northern China. This American presence was ended in September 1901 after the Boxer Protocol had been signed by China and 12 other countries. This agreement imposed severe penalties on China, including an indemnity of $739,000,000, the maintenance of a fortified legation quarter in Peking, and a protective allied garrison for the Peking-Tientsin railroad. The U.S. Army contributed to the latter until 1938.

The United States claimed only $25,000,000 from the indemnity, and in 1907 the administration realized that even this was more than enough to compensate American citizens for losses in the Boxer Rebellion. Accordingly, some $17,000,000 was returned to China, which used the sum to establish a trust for the education of Chinese Nationals in the United States as well as China.

The four years spanning the turn of the century· had been momentous for the United States and its armed forces. The Spanish-American War had projected the United States onto the world stage as a major diplomatic and military power with the ability to use its strength over trans-oceanic distances, and also signaled the nation's interest in imperialist ambition. American involvement in the allied response to the Boxer Rebellion confirmed this interest, although the removal of most American forces after the relief of the legations also revealed the distinctly limited nature of the country's aspirations. The Boxer Rebellion also marked the first American involvement in allied military ventures.

A new era

The first years of the 20th century were a period of change for the United States.

Boxers captured and brought into Tientsin by the 6th Cavalry Regiment.

Within domestic politics, these years marked the beginning of the "progressive era," when a peaceful, if hard-fought, revolution was waged by political leaders such as President Theodore Roosevelt to solve the related social and economic problems springing from the huge growth of industry at the end of the 19th century. This revolution was fought by politicians who saw a combination of legislation and administrative measures as the means to secure a new and more democratic order for the people of the United States, and was ably supported by social reformers and the influential writings of the so-called "muckrakers."

Within those American circles concerned with American diplomacy and foreign relations, the major problems were seen as the adjustment of American institutions and policies to take account of the United States' newfound position as a world power. Immediately after the end of the Spanish-American War, there had been a tendency to revert to a traditional isolationist foreign policy, but more farsighted thinkers saw that such a policy had been made impossible by the American possession of the Philippines, continued unrest of the Caribbean, and the worldwide growth of American trade.

Politicians and military men were also aware that there was now a compelling reason for foreign policy to be matched by a military establishment geared for intervention if necessary, and the period between the Boxer Rebellion and the entry of the United States into World War I was marked by a considerable modification of the established order in the army and navy.

This was a period of steadily intensifying rivalry between the great powers, as a complex network of diplomatic and military alliances slowly straitened them into two antagonistic blocs. The United States' geographical isolation and diplomatic neutrality held the country aloof from these "entangling alliances," but the country nonetheless strengthened and modernized its forces. The navy would be the United States' first line of defense in any world conflict, so it was only sensible to give this service the lion's share of available funding.

An Improved Navy

The excellent performance of the navy

The Chinese
authorities responded
quickly to the success
of the allied expedition
in northern China, and
Boxer suspects were
quickly brought to
Chinese justice.

of a canal across the Panamanian isthmus of Colombia, thereby creating a shorter route between the Atlantic and Pacific than the long haul around South America. At the same time, the modernization of the navy that had been started in the 1880s was pressed ahead with considerable vigor in the first part of this century. President Theodore Roosevelt's administrations between 1901 and 1909 inherited a healthy shipbuilding program from McKinley's term. A momentum built up that was slowed only partially (and then mainly by the demands of increasing technological sophistication) in the administration of President William H. Taft between 1909 and 1913, and in the first administration of President Woodrow Wilson between 1913 and 1917. In short, by 1917 the U.S. Navy was second in power only to the navies of the United Kingdom and Germany.

The main harbinger of the navy's greater strength was the battleship, with its substantial battery of large-caliber guns arranged in turrets along the centerline so that they could be moved onto either beam. Generally known as the "dreadnought" after the first such battleship, the British H.M.S. *Dreadnought* completed in 1906, the type was already under development in the United States at the time of the *Drednought's* appearance. The first to be completed were two ships of the "South Carolina" class with eight 12-inch guns, followed by four similar ships of the "Delaware" and "Florida" classes, two ships of the "Wyoming" class with twelve 12-inch guns, and two ships of the "New York" class with ten 14-inch guns. They were powerful modern ships, but expert criticism in 1908 suggested that the ships had their armor belt too low on the hull, sat too low in the water to fight with all their guns in any sort of heavy sea, and had poor protection against the torpedo boats which most navies were building as a counter to expensive battleships. This criticism resulted in the delivery from 1911 of the so-called "all or nothing" type of battleship which had superb protection but a slight sacrifice of speed. The first of these were two "Nevada" class ships with ten 14-inch guns in two triple and two twin turrets, and four ships

in the Spanish-American War, and thus its political popularity, was of course an important factor in gaining financial support from Congress. Men such as Theodore Roosevelt and Senator Henry Cabot Lodge of Massachusetts called for a navy second in size and power only to that of the United Kingdom, and Congress obliged with the necessary legislation and funds.

Within the navy itself, one of the most important results of the Spanish-American War had been the acquisition of operating bases in the Caribbean and the Pacific. Certainly the availability of Guantanamo Bay in Cuba and other bases in the area helped the development of American power into the Caribbean, but in the longer term, the bases in the Philippines and Guam proved more important in allowing American naval power to operate effectively across the Pacific.

In the shorter term, the navy realized that it lacked the ships and men to add a real Pacific power to its Atlantic and Caribbean capabilities. Yet such power was important if the United States was to retain the Philippines and build on the possibilities offered. One solution to this problem was the creation

Panama Canal
For further references
see pages
92, 93, 122

The first true machine-gun adopted by the U.S. Army was the 0·3-inch caliber Maxim Model 1904, but for financial reasons only a relatively small number were bought. Other machine-guns were later produced in modest numbers for the army, but the first one bought in significant quantities was the 0·3-inch Browning Model 1917 (or M1917), a development of the Model 1901. The weapon was recoil-operated with water cooling and could therefore sustain a rate of fire of between 450 and 600 rounds per minute for long periods. This made the weapon an excellent medium machine-gun in the sustained-fire role when it was installed on the standard 53·15-pound tripod mounting and fed with ammunition from 250-round fabric or disintegrating metal-link belts. The gun weighed 41 pounds with water, was 38·5 inches long, and fired its projectiles with a muzzle velocity of 2,800 feet per second.

of the "Pennsylvania" and "New Mexico" classes with twelve 14-inch guns in four triple turrets. The displacement of these battleships rose from 16,000 to 32,000 tons, while speed increased from 18.5 knots on the 16,500 horsepower of two reciprocating steam engines to 21 knots on the 32,000 horsepower of four geared steam turbines.

Over the same period, the navy also introduced substantial numbers of the type known as destroyers. They were derived from the torpedo boat, but had a larger hull so that guns as well as torpedoes could be carried. The ships had high performance and served in the twin roles of torpedo boat and torpedo boat destroyer. Another innovation of the period was the submarine.

Limited Modernization of the Army

The army had not been as successful as the navy in the Spanish-American War, and the high command recognized that in addition to organizational failings, there were severe equipment deficiencies. An obvious first step was the replacement of the 1892 Krag-Jorgensen rifle and its flimsy rod-type bayonet with a thoroughly

The Philippine Insurrection showed the U.S. Army that it needed a modern pistol offering a high rate of fire and firing a truly man-stopping projectile. The result was the army's first semi-automatic pistol, the classic 0·45-inch caliber Colt M1911A1. This recoil-operated handgun weighs 2·43 pounds, has a seven-round detachable box magazine in the grip, and fires its heavy projectile with a muzzle velocity of 830 feet per second.

modern bolt-action, magazine-fed rifle in the form of the Springfield Model 1903 rifle that was complemented after 1905 by a sturdy 16-inch knife bayonet. After 1906 it used a ·30-06 inch cartridge with a greater propellant load to give the bullet a higher muzzle velocity, which produced a flatter and more accurate trajectory and greater hitting power at any given range. Experience in the Philippine campaigns had revealed the need for a neater yet harder-hitting handgun than the 0·38-inch caliber revolver, and the superlative 0·45-inch caliber Colt Model 1911 semi-automatic pistol was adopted.

The army was less farsighted with the machine-gun, which was shown in World War I to be a decisive weapon. Right up to the Spanish-American War, the army had used the large, heavy Gatling gun, which was a hand-cranked weapon. Yet despite the fact that the "modern" machine-gun was invented by an American, Hiram Maxim, and then produced in two of its earliest definitive forms by another two Americans, John Browning and Isaac Lewis, it was the European powers that adopted the machine-gun as a major weapon. Between 1898 and 1916, American machine-gun procurement allowed each National Guard and regular regiment to receive only one and four machine-guns respectively. In 1916, the army finally accepted the need for much larger numbers of machine-guns.

The same basic pattern was followed in artillery procurement. Production of black powder was finally abandoned in favor of smokeless nitrocellulose propellants. In 1902, the army did adopt a new 3-inch gun as its standard field weapon, a modestly advanced design with an advanced recoil mechanism. In overall terms, the design and production of American field artillery were inferior to

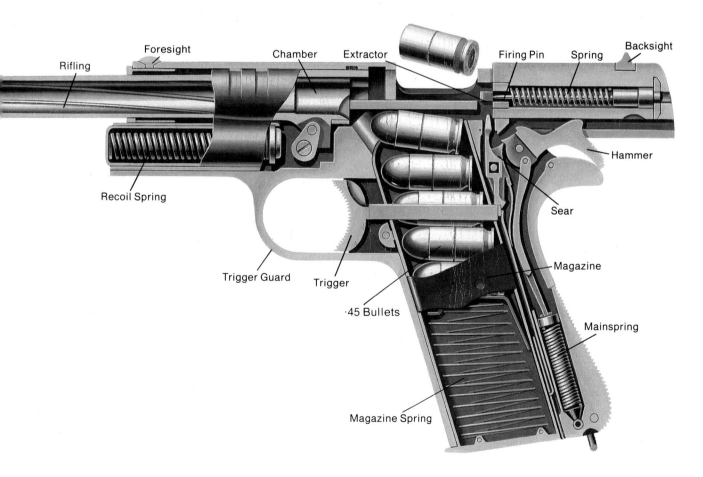

Rifling — Foresight — Chamber — Extractor — Firing Pin — Spring — Backsight — Hammer — Sear — Magazine — Mainspring — Magazine Spring — ·45 Bullets — Trigger — Trigger Guard — Recoil Spring

Elihu Root
For further references
see pages
84, 85, 86, *87*

those of the European powers. Considerable effort was also expended on the development of coast artillery as a means of keeping open those major American ports that might be blockaded and attacked by enemy ships.

These equipment changes were matched by modification of the army's basic organization and administration to overcome the defects that had been revealed so glaringly in the Spanish-American War. The spur to this comparatively rapid change was not so much the army's realization of its own

Monthly Pay of U.S. Enlisted Army Personnel in 1907

Sergeant Major and Quartermaster Sergeant of Engineer Corps	$36
Ordnance Sergeant and Sergeant of Engineer Corps	$34
Hospital Stewards (First Class)	$30
Sergeant Major and Quartermaster Sergeant of Cavalry, Artillery and Infantry	$23
Principal Musician, Chief Trumpeter, Saddler Sergeant, Hospital Steward (Second Class), First Sergeant (Cavalry, Artillery and Infantry)	$22
Corporals of Engineer and Ordnance Corps Hospital Steward (Third Class)	$20
Sergeants of Cavalry, Artillery and Infantry First Class Privates of Engineer and Ordnance Corps	$17
Saddler, Farrier, Corporals of Cavalry, Artillery and Infantry	$15
Musician, Trumpeter, Second Class Privates of Engineer and Ordnance, Privates of Cavalry, Artillery and Infantry	$13

limitations, but a public perception that the easy American land victory in the recent war was based on Spanish incompetence not American skill.

The Reforms of Elihu Root

A presidential committee of investigation, headed by Major General Granville M. Dodge, soon showed the need for reform of the army's high command, and elimination of inefficiency at all levels in the War Department. This was music to the ear of Elihu Root, a New York lawyer appointed as Secretary of War in 1899. His appointment reflected McKinley's belief that the new overseas possessions would bring a host of legal problems. Root himself, however, saw his main task as a thorough reform of the army. As this former corporate lawyer put it: "The men who have combined various corporations...which we call trusts, have reduced the costs of production and have increased their efficiency by doing the very same thing we propose (Congress) shall do now, and it does seem a pity that the Government of the United States should be the only great industrial establishment that cannot profit by the lessons which the world of industry and of commerce has learned to such good effect."

Root took expert advice, and from 1899 on, he published a series of telling reports on his proposed reform of the army's organization and institutions. As a first step, Root made sure that his "bible," an unfinished manuscript by Colonel Emory Upton, was published in 1904 as The Military Policy of the United States. It helped to condition opinion toward Root's preferred solution of a strong but expandable regular army as the cornerstone of the American military establishment. Root was convinced that the army's task was "to provide for war," and therefore set about molding the army into an instrument capable of meeting the demand of modern warfare and still able to serve the interests of national power. The core of Root's plan was to integrate the bureaux of the War Department, and also the various elements of the regular army, the National Guard, and the volunteers.

Corporal, Peking Legation Guard, U.S. Marine Corps, 1900

The guard for the U.S. Legation in Peking was provided by 56 marines and sailors from the battleship U.S.S. *Oregon* and the cruiser U.S.S. *Newark*. In the siege of the legations, these Americans fought in "shirt sleeve" order because of the heat, and the khaki campaign hat had the bronze U.S. Marine Corps badge on the left side of the crown. This marine is seen in service dress, with a dark blue tunic, light blue slacks, and black leather campaign equipment. The tunic had a blue collar trimmed in red, red piping down the front and along the bottom seam, and blue cuff sashes trimmed in red; the chevron strips were outlined in red. The inch-wide red stripe on the outer seam of the pants was worn only by noncommissioned and commissioned officers. The weapon is the M1898 Krag-Jorgensen rifle.

The heart of the connected organizational and administrative problem, Root decided, was the long standing division of authority between the Secretary of War and the Commanding General of the Army. The former, working through his various bureau heads, was responsible for administration and finances, while the latter was responsible for discipline and control of troops in the field. Root planned to remove this division of authority and reduce the independence of the bureau heads, and suggested the replacement of the commanding general by a chief of staff who would advise the president and execute the president's wishes via the secretary of war.

Chief of Staff and General Staff

In the Spanish-American War, the army had also failed in the field of long-term planning. Root planned to over-

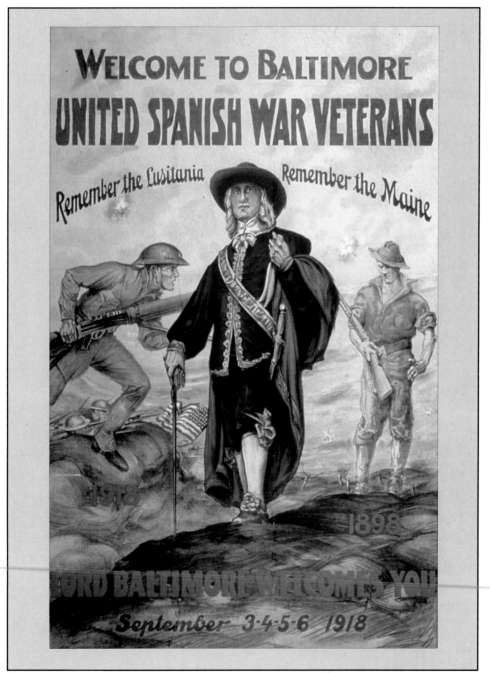

The Spanish-American War continued to exercise a considerable hold on the popular imagination for many years, as indicated by this 1918 poster for a reunion of Spanish-American War veterans.

come this failing by creating a general staff, made up of a group of officers devoted exclusively to military planning. Root argued that planning failures in earlier wars had happened because the task was being dropped suddenly on commanders already weighed down by other responsibilities. Congressional approval was needed for the creation of such a body, and the secretary paved the way for it in 1901 by appointing a War College Board to become a pioneer general staff.

By 1903, Congress had agreed to most of Root's recommendations, which provided the legislation for both the chief of staff and the General Staff. However, it refused to allow the consolidation of the various War Department bureaux. Even so, Congress had provided Root with the framework creating a more efficient army. But though the framework now existed, there was considerable opposition from army officers, many congressmen, and a large part of the concerned public, all of which would have to be overcome before the full range of Root's eminently practical reforms could be implemented.

Root decided that the best way to secure acceptance of his ideas was through infiltration, starting with the army's officer corps. This was one of the major reasons for the establishment in 1903 of the Army War College, where army officers would hopefully come to understand the problems of the War Department and of senior command in the field. As it happened, however, the Army War College concerned itself mainly with war planning, and so became a virtual tool of the General Staff.

The General Staff itself was something of a failure in its first years, for it became bogged down in administration. Even so, some useful results emerged, and as it slowly began to emerge from its administrative morass, its officers began to appreciate the organization's real functions and powers. The decisive moment came with the appointment of Major General Leonard Wood as chief of staff in 1906. Wood reorganized the General Staff along the lines that Root had wanted, cutting administration and directing his officers' energies toward planning. There was still internal as well as exter-

nal opposition, but matters improved dramatically after Wood and Henry L. Stimson, the Secretary of War between 1911 and 1913, managed to oust their chief opponent, Major General Fred C. Ainsworth, the adjutant general.

Revised Army School System

During the Spanish-American War, all the army's schools had been closed to provide additional officers for expeditionary forces and the army detachments left in the United States. Root took advantage of the closures to revise the army school system according to the philosophy embodied in the Army War College and General Staff, which was to improve the standard of the army's professional training. After considerable thought, the War Department ordered in 1901 that the schools for the training of army officers were to be the Military Academy at West Point, the five service schools (the Artillery School, Engineer School of Application, School of Submarine Defense, School of Application for Cavalry and Field Artillery, and Army Medical School), the General Staff and Service College at Fort Leavenworth, the War College, and a school of theory and practice at each post of elementary instruction. The tasks of the Fort Leavenworth school were now the training of officers in combined-arms operations, and their preparation for staff and command positions in large units.

The continued development of the army's weapons and operating principles meant that additional schools were soon needed, and in 1905, the Signal School was added, followed in 1911 by the Field Artillery School and in 1913 by the School of Musketry.

While the creation of the chief of staff and General Staff, together with their supporting organizations, was the most important result of Root's reforms of the army, there were also a number of smaller but still important changes designed to keep the army up to date. For example, the Medical Department established separate Medical, Hospital, Army Nurse, Dental, and Medical Reserve Corps. Congress agreed in 1907 that the artillery should be divided into the Coast

Artillery Corps and the Field Artillery, and in 1912, it followed one of Root's recommendations to consolidate the Subsistence and Pay Departments with the Quartermaster Department to form the Quartermaster Corps. The 1912 legislation also established an enlisted service corps, which provided at last for the use of specialist servicemen, rather than a combination of civilians and combat troop details, for this important task.

In the period immediately after the Spanish-American War, about one-third of the regular army served overseas.

A recruiting poster for the U.S. Marine Corps emphasizes the corps' role as seaborne soldiers.

Most of these men were posted to the Philippines, first to fight the insurrection and then to provide the garrison forces that also rooted out the last rebel elements and trained the Philippine Scouts. Other regular soldiers were stationed in Alaska, China, Hawaii, and elsewhere. Between 1902 and 1911, the army therefore had extensive overseas commitments as well as the task of protecting the United States itself. At the same time, its average strength was only 75,000 officers and men from an establishment figure of 100,000 fixed by Congress in 1902 as the strength for 30 infantry and 15 cavalry regiments supported by a corps of artillery.

The Volunteer Forces Updated

To make up for the regular establishment's small overall strength,

and also to set right some of the defects revealed by the Spanish-American War, the War Department planned a reorganization of the volunteer forces. As might be expected, Root took the lead, and in 1901 the secretary of war presented to Congress a plan to reform the National Guard. The first result was a 1903 act to reform the completely obsolete Militia Act of 1792. Based on the Dick bill, the new act split the militia into two types, namely the Organized Militia (to be known as the National Guard) and the Reserve Militia. The act also dictated that, over a five-year period, the National Guard should be revised in organization and equipment to mirror the regular army. The act provided the funding for this major alteration and stipulated that the National Guard should drill at least twice each month and also undertake a short annual training period, that regular officers could be seconded to the

Marines on patrol on Nicaragua during 1912, when their task was internal policing of this poor country.

The American forces always found recruitment difficult in times of peace; in periods of crisis, all branches of the service were flooded by would-be soldiers and sailors.

National Guard, and that joint maneuvers should be held each year.

The act was on the right lines with these requirements for the National Guard, but it failed to remove the constraints that had long restricted the federal power to call out and to control the personnel of the National Guard. Later legislation, in 1908 and 1914, removed some of these limitations by giving the president the right to decide the length of federal service required, and with senate advice and consent, to appoint all officers while the National Guard was employed in federal service.

A Divisional Organization

The Spanish-American War and observation of developments in European armies also convinced the army of the need for large, self-sufficient units as the basic fighting formations for major field operations. The regiment remained the largest unit in the army's peacetime establishment, but the *Field Service Regulations*, issued by the General Staff in 1905, laid the foundations for wartime divisions composed of integrated and self-supporting units. In 1910, the General Staff went one stage further and planned for three permanent infantry divisions based on specific regular and National Guard regiments. Because of problems along the frontier with Mexico in 1911, the implementation of this plan was postponed. Instead, the General Staff ordered the creation of a provisional maneuver division (13,000 men in three brigades plus supporting units) at San Antonio, Texas, where its presence was designed to quell border disturbances.

The assembly of the provisional maneuver division was a salutary lesson to the General Staff in the problems of mobilizing such a formation, for it took several months to gather the required regular units from posts all over the United States. And despite the virtual stripping of every depot and arsenal, the division still lacked much of its required equipment. Even when the division was finally assembled in August 1911, it could scarcely be considered operational, as none of its regiments was at full strength, let alone fully supplied with weapons and other equipment.

Luckily, the division was not actually needed for military action; and shortly after it had reached its peak strength, the division was dissolved and its units sent back to their home stations. The army wanted to relocate units for a greater concentration of troops in fewer areas, but this plan was halted by congressmen who were unwilling to see army posts in their districts closed down. The army instead had to organize itself on paper so that the men of each post, averaging 700 soldiers, could rapidly join one of the three planned divisions if necessary. This effort provided worthwhile in 1913, when another bout of troubled relations with Mexico was followed by the assembly of a division in Texas in less than a week.

Continued Commitments in the Caribbean

As these administrative and organizational matters were being tackled, the army was still involved in the Caribbean. The formal end of the Spanish-American War had not brought instant peace and stability to newly independent Cuba. The Teller amendment had guaranteed that the United States could have no territorial ambitions toward Cuba, but decades of Spanish misrule and a decade of fighting meant that the condition of the country was dreadful. Humanitarian reasons alone were more than enough to keep the army involved in a program designed to give the Cubans at least the basis of political and economic stability.

The first step was the establishment of central authority, and a provisional government was established under Major General John R. Brooke, who was later succeeded by General Wood. Once it had been established, the provisional government set itself the initial task of rehabilitating and reforming the country, including as a vital first step the elimination of yellow fever, which army research had shown to be transmitted by a particular type of mosquito.

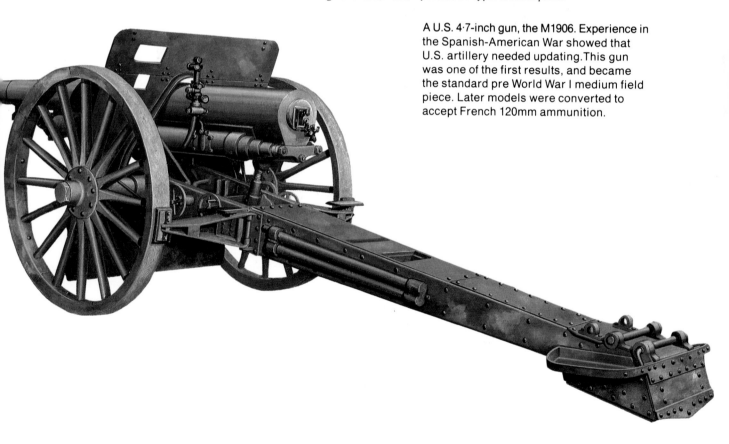

A U.S. 4·7-inch gun, the M1906. Experience in the Spanish-American War showed that U.S. artillery needed updating. This gun was one of the first results, and became the standard pre World War I medium field piece. Later models were converted to accept French 120mm ammunition.

Marines prepare to embark for the Haitian expedition in August 1912.

With these essential first tasks in hand and order restored to the country, the provisional government ordered a constituent assembly to discuss the new nation's basic law as the foundation of a republican constitution. At American insistence, this law included provisions (known as the Platt amendment and carried over into the 1903 treaty between Cuba and the United States) to limit the amount of foreign debt Cuba could incur, to grant the United States naval bases at Guantanamo and Bahia Honda, and to give the United States the right to intervene when Cuban independence or civil rights were threatened. In 1902 the Cubans held their first elections, and after the island nation's first president had been inaugurated, the U.S. Army left the country.

The Army of Cuban Pacification

Given the centuries of Spanish rule, a long tradition of resistance to central authority, and the short time in which Cuba had sought to evolve a practical democracy, it is hardly surprising that there were difficulties. By late 1906, these problems had reached the point of rebellion against the central government, and Secretary of War Taft urged President Roosevelt that the time was more than ripe for American intervention under the terms of the Platt amendment. Roosevelt agreed, and a force of five infantry regiments, two cavalry regiments, and several batteries of field artillery were sent as the Army of Cuban Pacification. This force quickly restored order without trouble or incident of any type, and was finally evacuated early in 1909. A similar operation had to be mounted again in 1912, and in 1917 a Cuban rebellion resulted in the despatch to Santiago of another American expeditionary force, which remained in Cuba between February and March of that year, and was again successful in restoring order. It was only in May 1934, after the adoption of its "Good Neighbor Policy," that the United States finally gave up its right to intervene in Cuba under the terms of the Platt amendment.

Intervention in Honduras and Nicaragua

The period between the turn of the century

and the United States' entry into World War I during April 1917 was marked by a number of similar interventions in Central America and the Caribbean. In January 1912, men of the Marine Corps landed in Honduras to protect American lives and property in the turbulent conditions that followed the 1911 end of the civil war, which had flared in 1909 after the country's defeat by Nicaragua in a short war between February and December 1907. In July 1912, marines were rushed to Nicaragua, where a civil war was raging: the marines stopped the hostilities and made sure that elections were held.

The Marines in Haiti...

As a far-sighted and energetic Secretary of War, Elihu Root played a key part in the development of the modern U.S. Army.

Three years later, in 1915, the marines were again needed to quell unrest, this time in the Caribbean nation of Haiti. This turmoil resulted from the turbulence of local politics at a time when several European nations were pressing the

country for the settlement of debts. The marines landed on July 3, and a protectorate was declared on September 1916. The marines quietened the situation and organized a Haitian constabulary which gradually assumed the task of policing the country. However, in 1918 the country revolted against the continued American occupation, and it was 1919 before the resulting disorder was suppressed. The marines remained in Haiti until August 1934, when arrangements were finally concluded between the United States and the Haitian assembly for the evacuation of these last American forces.

...and in the Dominican Republic

In 1916, the situation in the neighboring Dominican Republic deteriorated sharply, and the collapse of internal order threatened to destroy the country's already poor economy. In May, men of the Marine Corps landed; and in their wake, American officials arrived to take

91

over the running of the Dominican Republic's economy. The situation continued to get worse, however, and on November 29, a full American occupation of the country was launched. This brought peace and stability to the Dominican Republic, and American forces were finally withdrawn in 1924.

The first years of the present century were also marked by increased American interest in a canal across one of the narrower parts of the Central American isthmus between the Gulf of Mexico and the Pacific Ocean. There had been many suggestions for such a canal over the years, and American enthusiasm had been sparked forcibly by the discovery of gold in California during 1848. The resulting rush of prospectors and those eager to exploit them had helped pave the way for the development of an overland route to the Pacific coast, but most of the traffic was carried by ships that had to pass around Cape Horn in a slow, long, and potentially dangerous sea journey.

Clearly, a passage through an isthmian canal would be considerably quicker,

shorter, and less dangerous. For this reason, therefore, the United States took a keen interest in various efforts to create a canal. The one that came closest to success was attempted in the 1880s by Ferdinand Lesseps, the French engineer who had created the Suez Canal. At the strategic rather than economic level, the need for an isthmian canal was highlighted during the Spanish-American War by the long journey of the battleship *Oregon*. She was detached from the Pacific Squadron to reinforce the North Atlantic Squadron at the beginning of the war, but only reached her new command just in time to participate in the final destruction of Cervera's squadron during the naval Battle of Santiago: the journey around Cape Horn from Puget Sound, Washington, to Cuba had taken the battleship 66 days.

Building the Panama Canal

Shortly after the end of the Spanish-American War, McKinley informed Con-

Construction work in progress on one of the Panama Canal's several sets of locks. Controlled by the Corps of Engineers, the building of the Panama Canal was an enormous political, military, and engineering achievement.

The Panama Canal was designed to accommodate the widest beam ships then operated and planned by the U.S. Navy. It was only in the later stages of World War II that the latest battleships became too wide to pass through the canal.

gress that an American-controlled isthmian canal was "now more than ever indispensable." In 1901, the United States and the United Kingdom signed the Hay-Pauncefote treaty. It overruled the 1850 Clayton-Bulwer treaty, which laid down equal American and British involvement in the construction and operation of any isthmian canal. Over the years, there had been great debate about whether the canal should pass through Nicaragua or the Panama province of Colombia; in 1903, the argument was decided in favor of Panama, the shorter route of the two options.

The United States offered to buy Panama from Colombia, but the offer was rejected on October 31, 1903. On November 3, Panama rebelled against Colombia. The presence of American warships off Panama hindered Colombian efforts to suppress the uprising. On November 6, the United States recognized the independence of Panama and, just four days later, accepted as the Panamanian ambassador to the United States Philippe Bunau-Varilla, who had been involved in the previous Panama Canal Company.

On November 18, the United States agreed to lease from the new republic of Panama the strip of land ten miles wide that became the Panama Canal Zone, to buy the surviving property of the French canal company of the 1880s, and to build, maintain, and operate a

Continued on page 122

Right: U.S. Marine Corps artillery in action during the Haitian intervention.

Below: Artillery was used relatively rarely in Haiti, and operations against Haitian bandits used patrols, such as the one photographed here during 1919, much more widely. The officer (left) carries a 0·45-inch Colt M1911 pistol, and with the exception of the man carrying a 0·3-inch Lewis light machine-gun (center right), the men are armed with 0·3-inch Springfield M1903 rifles.

Above: U.S. Marine dispatch riders with their motorcycles in Haiti. The lack of a widespread telephone network made such riders indispensable.

Left: U.S. Marines in Haiti with a light armored car.

Brigadier General, U.S. Army, 1914

All mounted officers of the U.S. Army wore breeches and boots in full dress order. The sash was used to indicate rank among general officers: major generals wore the sash across the torso from the right shoulder to the left side, but not extended around the waist. The sword is the standard M1903 officer's saber, which was carried by all commissioned officers.

THE U.S. NAVY FROM 1815 TO 1860

The launch of the *Washington* at Portsmouth Navy Yard on October 1, 1814. This ship was part of the U.S. Navy's expansion under Commodore Isaac Hull, whose long career included command of the Boston, Portsmouth, New Hampshire, and Washington navy yards.

Just eight days after Congress had ratified the treaty that ended the War of 1812, both houses followed the advice of President James Madison and declared war on Algiers on March 2, 1815. This small but fascinating conflict, the fifth war that the young United States had fought in 40 years in support of its seaborne trade, provides telling evidence that the United States was extremely "sea minded" from the beginning of its history.

Even as the War of 1812 ended, American ports were preparing for the return of peace. On their wharves and in their warehouses lay the fruits of two productive years, and European mouths and industries were eager for food and raw materials such as cotton. In the year after the end of the War of 1812, the value of American exports soared from $7 to $53 million. Imports rose even more steeply – from $13 to $113 million. The period after the War of 1812 saw the first true blossoming of U.S. trade on a virtually global basis. The only problem occurred in the Mediterranean, where the hostility, and the greed of the Dey of Algiers, the Bey of Tunis, and the Pasha of Tripoli on the Barbary Coast led to a war against these "Barbary pirates."

The War of 1812 had revealed the navy's lack of adequate ships. A postwar construction program added several important new craft, most notably the 74-gun ships of the line *Franklin*, *Independence*, and *Washington*, the 44-gun frigates *Guerriere* and *Java*, six sloops, and several smaller vessels. The navy organized two squadrons for the campaign against the rulers of the Barbary Coast. The first sailed on May 20, 1815, under Commodore Stephen Decatur. It included the frigates *Guerriere*, *Constellation*, and *Macedonian*, the sloops *Epervier* (18 guns) and *Ontario* (16 guns), the 14-gun brigs *Firefly*, *Spark*, and *Flambeau*, and the 12-gun schooners *Torch* and *Spitfire*. The second squadron, under Commodore William Bainbridge, included the ship of the line *Independence*, the frigates *United States* and *Congress*, the 18-gun sloop *Erie*, the 14-gun brigs *Chippewa*, *Saranac*, *Boxer*, and *Enterprise*, and the six-gun schooner *Lynx*.

Decatur in the Mediterranean

Decatur sailed first to Cadiz in southern Spain and then to Tangiers in North Africa. There, he discovered that the Algerine fleet had re-entered the Mediterranean after cruising in the Atlantic. Decatur scattered his squadron in search of the enemy, and on June 17 the Algerine flagship, *Mashuda* (46 guns), was encountered off Cap de Gat and engaged in succession by the *Constellation*, *Ontario*, *Guerriere*, and *Epervier*. After 20 of her crew had been killed and many more wounded, the *Mashuda* surrendered. American losses were four killed and ten wounded, most of them caused by the bursting of a gun on the *Guerriere*.

Two days later, off Cape Palos, the 22-gun Algerine brig *Estedio* was driven

Left: Stephen Decatur was another major figure in the early part of the existence of the U.S. Navy.

Opposite Top: On February 16, 1804, Lieutenant Stephen Decatur sailed into Tripoli harbor and burned the frigate *Philadelphia*. The ship used by Decatur and his 80 volunteers was the ketch *Intrepid*. It had previously been the Tripolitanian vessel *Mastico* that was captured on December 23 of the year before by Decatur in the 12-gun schooner *Enterprise*.

Opposite Below: The U.S. Navy bombarded Tripoli on five occasions, but such efforts generally had little effect on shore fortifications. The Americans were informed by their diplomatic intermediary in the city, the French consul Bonaventure Beaussier, that Pasha Yusuf Karamanli was wholly unimpressed.

Pirates were a constant worry to U.S. trade ships, and they eventually became troublesome enough to cause the U.S. Navy to get involved in action against them. A boarding party from the *Enterprise* sets out toward a Tripolitanian pirate ship (left).

ashore by the *Epervier, Spark, Torch,* and *Spitfire.* Many of the crew escaped in boats, but the Americans captured 80 and discovered 23 dead on the stranded ship.

Decatur then assembled his squadron and sailed to Algiers, where peace negotiations began on June 29. The Dey wasted as much time as he could, and only when Decatur threatened to capture the rest of the Algerine navy did the Algerine ruler reluctantly agree to Decatur's terms. Decatur then sailed to Tunis and Tripoli, and when Bainbridge's

squadron arrived, the Americans imposed terms on the two rulers. The two squadrons rendezvoused at Gibraltar in September 1815 and sailed for home after detaching Captain John Shaw with the *United States, Constellation, Erie,* and *Ontario* to guard American interests in the Mediterranean.

In April, 1816, the Dey refused to ratify the resulting treaty and instead proposed a return to an earlier arrangement agreed in 1795 whereby the U.S. paid a tribute to guarantee the safety of their ships off the North African coast. As Shaw was seeking

After the failure of his bombardment against Tripoli, Preble decided to destroy the Tripolitanian flotilla by sailing an explosive-filled vessel into the harbor and exploding her there. The vessel selected was the *Intrepid*, and on September 3, 1804, the vessel was sailed into the harbor by 13 volunteers (one lieutenant, two midshipmen, and ten seamen). The idea was for the crew to set fire to the vessel in a place well away from the powder charge while the ship was on course for the enemy flotilla, and then to escape in small boats. For reasons that are still unknown, the *Intrepid* blew up in the entrance to the harbor, killing everyone on board, at 9:47 p.m.

instructions, a combined British and Dutch fleet arrived off Algiers in August 1816, bombarded the city, and virtually destroyed the Algerine navy.

Continued American Presence in the Mediterranean

There was thus no way in which the Algerines could check Commodore Isaac Chauncey when this American officer, commanding the *Washington*, arrived off the city in December 1816 with a large squadron. The Dey agreed a final peace, but was assassinated nine months later. Conditions in the Mediterranean did become less volatile, but for several years, a U.S. squadron was maintained in the Mediterranean.

During this period, the navy was also involved closer to home in the suppression of piracy in the Caribbean. As early as the period between 1806 and 1810, American gunboats had played an active part in suppressing the activities of buccaneers and European privateers around the mouth of the Mississippi River. In October 1814, just three months before the Battle of New Orleans, a joint expedition under the command of Commodore Daniel T. Patterson and Colonel

Ross finally destroyed a pirate haven at Barataria, capturing 12 ships that were later condemned as prizes.

The end of the War of 1812 put a stop to European privateering, but soon privateering off the Louisiana coast by ships flying the flags of newly independent Colombia, Mexico, and Venezuela began. The period also saw a very rapid expansion of trade from New Orleans and the new U.S. possessions on the northern side of the Gulf of Mexico to the West Indies and across the Caribbean. As early as 1818, New Orleans was the second most important American port for exports; by 1834, it had become the most important. Other ports grew up along the southern coast of the United States, and their trade became an irresistible lure for pirates operating between the Bahamas and South America. Between 1815 and 1823, there were nearly 3,000 reported cases of piracy in the area. Many of them involved murder and torture as well as robbery.

Naval Legislation

On March 3, 1819, Congress passed legislation that materially affected the navy. First, rules about naming warships stipulated that ships of the line were to be named after states, frigates after rivers, and sloops after cities. Second, authorization was given to step up the war against the pirates, who were capturing hundreds of American ships every year. The worst area for piracy was the Caribbean, and the new law gave permission for the navy to escort merchant convoys and recapture ships taken by pirates. Third, the president was authorized to use the navy to suppress the West African slave trade.

In 1823, the navy established a West India Squadron to deal with the serious threat to lives and property. Commanded by Commodore James Biddle, the squadron included the frigates *Macedonian* and *Congress*, the sloops *Cyane*, *John Adams*, *Hornet*, and *Peacock*, the brigs *Spark* and *Enterprise*, the schooners *Alligator*, *Grampus*, *Shark*, and *Porpoise*, and the gunboats *No. 158* (or *Revenge*) and *No. 168*.

Operations Against Caribbean Pirates

The work of combating the pirates was extremely difficult. In addition to the normal hazards of naval service and operations in the tropics, there was also a higher incidence of frequently fatal tropical disease. Yellow fever was especially prevalent among the crews of the open boats that used to scout hidden bays and lagoons.

Commodore David Porter made his name as the head of the West India Squadron, which helped to curtail the activities of pirates off the southern coast of the United States during the 1820s.

Below: On January 1/2, 1839, ships of Commodore George C. Read's East India Squadron bombarded the Sumatra villages of Muckee and Quallah Battoo (Kuala Batu). The village had undergone a similar experience in 1832 at the hands of Captain John Downes's 44-gun frigate *Potomac* after a local attack on the merchantmen *Friendship*. In 1838, the locals murdered the captain of the merchantman *Eclipse*, and after a bombardment by the 44-gun frigate *Columbia* and 18-gun sloop *John Adams*, a 360-man landing was led by Commander T.W. Wyman.

In January 1822, a boat party from the *Porpoise*, under the command of Lieutenant Ramage, attacked a pirate haven near Bahia Honda in Cuba and destroyed nine vessels. Just two months later, a similar party from the *Enterprise* destroyed eight vessels and six smaller craft near Cabo San Antonio. The *Alligator* and *Grampus* also operated in Cuban waters, capturing several prizes in the process.

In August of the same year, the Grampus engaged the privateer *Palmyra* off Puerto Rico, and in just three and a half minutes, the privateer was a wreck. Operations continued off Cuba and Puerto Rico, notable events being in September, when the *Peacock* sank a pirate vessel off Bahia Honda, and two months later, when a boat party from the *Alligator* destroyed a pirate lair west of Matanzas and captured five pirate vessels, two of which turned out to be American vessels that had previously been captured by the pirates.

In 1823, command of the West India Squadron was assumed by Commodore David Porter, who established the squadron's much-needed operational base at Key West off the tip of Florida. The squadron was also reinforced by eight schooners, five barges, and the navy's second steamship, the first to serve as a warship. This vessel was the *Sea Gull*, which had been bought in December 1822. It was commissioned on February 14, 1823, under Lieutenant William H. Watson as a shallow-draft warship capable of operating against pirates along the Cuban coast.

Porter tried to enlist the support of the Spanish governor of Puerto Rico, but he was no more successful in real terms than Biddle had been with the governor of Cuba the year before. The West India Squadron made a major sweep between Santo Domingo and the Yucatan peninsula of Mexico, but encountered little pirate activity; the previous year's operations had curtailed most activity except off Puerto Rico.

In September 1823, a yellow fever epidemic swept through Key West, and most of the West India Squadron's ships were moved north into healthier climes until the following year. When they returned to the Caribbean, the ships continued their activities in much the same way as they had in 1823 and again found little pirate activity.

The Fajardo Incident

In November 1824, Porter responded with speed and strength to an incident on the eastern coast of Puerto Rico. When Lieutenant C.T. Platt, commanding the schooner *Beagle*, arrived in Fajardo to discuss the return of U.S. property apparently stolen from St. Thomas, the mayor of the town arrested him. Porter arrived on November 14 and promptly landed 200 men from the *John Adams*, *Beagle*, and *Grampus*. Porter informed the mayor that he left "entirely to your choice whether you come...or await my visit to your town. Should you decline coming to me, I shall take with me an armed force competent to punish the aggressors, and if any resistance is made, the total destruction of Fajardo is certain."

The mayor came out to meet Porter and apologized. The administration was unhappy with Porter's high-handed action, however, and recalled him for court martial. Porter was suspended from the navy for six months and resigned his commission. The new commander of the West India Squadron was Commodore Lewis Warrington.

In March 1825, the *Grampus* captured a pirate vessel after a 45-minute action off Ponce. In April, a pirate haven east of Matanzas was destroyed by a combined American and British expedition under an American commander, Lieutenant McKeever of the barge *Gallinipper*, effectively ending the pirate menace in the Caribbean, where some 65 pirate vessels had been captured. By 1829, the West India Squadron had been scaled down to small size.

During the same period, other sections of the navy had had similar results in waters as far distant as the east and west coasts of South America, the east coast of Africa, the Mediterranean, and China. Fighting was comparatively rare, for the threat of naval action was generally enough to deter would-be pirates and thereby guarantee the safety of American merchant shipping.

The other main threat to American merchant shipping during this time was the turbulence of the South American states as they threw off the colonial rule of Spain. One of the most celebrated naval episodes of this period was the voyage of the sloop *Ontario*, which sailed from New York in October 1817 under the command of Captain James Biddle. The ship's apparent task was to support merchant shipping off Brazil and Argentina, but her real object was to take formal possession of part of Oregon, which had just been relinquished by the British under the terms of the Treaty of Ghent.

American Interests in the Pacific

When the *Ontario* reached Valparaiso in Chile in January 1818, Biddle discovered that Chile had revolted against Spain. A Spanish army was moving south from Peru, and Valparaiso was blockaded by a Spanish squadron. In itself, this was of little importance to Biddle and J.B. Prevost, the diplomatic commissioner he was carrying to Oregon. However, the two men learned that several U.S. ships had been seized and their crews imprisoned. Early negotiations failed to secure the release of the ships and their crews, so while Biddle sailed off to complete the Oregon mission, Prevost remained in Chile and traveled to Oregon on a British warship later. Biddle and Prevost missed each other in the Pacific, but their warnings about the worsening situation on the western side of South America had alerted the U.S. government, which sent out the frigate *Macedonian* under Captain John Downes. She arrived off Chile during January 1819 and proved invaluable in her support of the merchant and whaling fleets in those waters.

In March 1821, the *Macedonian* was relieved by another frigate, Captain

Ridgely's *Constellation*, which was in turn relieved in the spring of 1822 by the ship of the line, Commodore Charles Stewart's *Franklin*, supported by the schooner *Dolphin*. These ships all played their part in allowing U.S. merchant ships to keep plying their trade, and this presence was maintained off the South American coast for many years to come.

Trade With Asia

Across the Pacific, trade with China and the Philippines was blossoming into a major commercial flower. There was considerable piracy in the area, however, and in May 1819 Captain J.D. Henley's *Congress* sailed from Hampton Roads, Virginia, on a pioneering journey to China. The ship traveled via Rio de Janeiro and the Cape of Good Hope, and reached the pirate-ridden Sunda Strait in September. The frigate then convoyed several U.S. merchant ships to Lintin Island at the mouth of the Pearl River, just downstream of the great Chinese port of Canton. Supplies were obtained only after considerable difficulty, as a bombardment from a British warship had stirred up the Chinese. In January 1820, the *Congress* became the first U.S. warship to reach the Philippine Islands, and it then returned to Lintin Island via the Sunda Strait. Supplies were even more difficult to obtain this time, and Henley had to make a show of force toward Canton before the Chinese would deliver the necessary stores. Hearing that there was a revolt in the Philippines, Henley sailed once more to the islands, where the presence of the *Congress* in Manila Bay helped to quieten the situation. The ship was then hit by cholera, and Henley decided to return to the United States. An outbreak of scurvy followed, and by the time the *Congress* reached Hampton Roads once more, in May 1821, the ship had lost 68 men.

Suppression of the Slave Trade

Another naval effort of the period was the suppression of the slave trade between

Slaves had to endure crowded and unhealthy conditions aboard slave traders' ships.

West Africa and the Americas. The first U.S. warship to reach the west coast of Africa was Captain Trenchard's sloop *Cyane*. She arrived early in 1820 and captured seven slaving vessels as she patrolled the region between the equator and the mouth of the Senegal River for almost a year. Later ships at this station were Captain G.C. Read's *Hornet*, which took one slaver, and Captain Wadsworth's *John Adams*. Other American warships involved in the area were Captain M.C. Perry's *Shark* and Captain R.F. Stockton's *Alligator*. The latter brought across the Atlantic a representative of the American Colonization Society. This man had been commissioned to choose a site for a colony of returned slaves, which eventually

became Liberia. The activities of these ships steadily reduced the potential of West Africa for U.S. slavers, and the brutal trade effectively died as a feature of commercial life.

These activities, begun at the end of the War of 1812, geared the navy into a pattern of support for merchant shipping interests. From 1823 until the outbreak of the Mexican War in 1846, this pattern was repeated and expanded as overseas trade grew by leaps and bounds. Typical of the continuing far-flung nature of naval operations was the despatch in 1825 of Commodore John Rodgers's *North Carolina*, a new ship of the line, to reinforce the squadron in the Mediterranean. British operations against Algiers and the revolt of Greece against Turkish rule had led to increased piracy in the Aegean Sea. Rodgers helped to secure the safety of American merchant shipping and negotiated a treaty with Turkey.

A similar situation arose off South America during 1826 when war broke out between Argentina and Brazil. The U.S. squadron in these waters was reinforced until the situation eased in 1829, and its continued presence proved useful in 1832, when the *Lexington* was detached to the Falkland Islands to prevent the harassment of American whalers.

Circumnavigations of the World

In 1825 Congress authorized the construction of a class of ten sloops, each displacing 700 tons and armed with 16 guns. On September 3, 1826, one of these vessels, Commander William B. Finch's *Vincennes*, left New York to become the first American naval vessel to circumnavigate the world before returning to New York on June 8, 1830.

Soon after the end of the *Vincennes* westward circumnavigation, a comparable voyage in the opposite direction was achieved by the frigate *Potomac* under Captain John Downes. The cause of the voyage was the slaughter, in February 1831, of many crewmen on the merchant ship *Friendship* by Sumatrans off Quallah Battoo on the west coast of the East Indian island. The *Potomac* sailed from New York via Cape Town and arrived off Quallah Battoo in February 1832 in the guise of a Danish merchant ship. A party of 282 sailors and marines was landed, and after heavy fighting, three of the forts were taken and the fourth destroyed by broadsides from the *Potomac*'s main battery. Quallah Battoo was then burned, and the local leaders asked for peace, promising that no further outrages would be committed against American ships. The *Potomac* then sailed via Java, Macao, Honolulu, Callao, and Cape Horn, arriving home in May 1834.

Another interesting voyage of the period was that of the schooner *Dolphin* under Captain Percival. This vessel was part of Commodore Isaac Hull's

squadron based at Callao in Peru for the protection of U.S. interests in the southeastern Pacific. Hull received word that the crew of a U.S. merchant ship, the *Globe*, had mutinied and taken refuge in the Musgrave Islands. Percival was despatched with orders to arrest the mutineers and visit other islands in the area.

The *Dolphin* sailed via the Galapagos and Marquesas islands, and reached the Musgraves in November 1825. Percival found only two of the mutineers; the others had been killed by the islanders or fled by boat. Percival ordered the islanders not to attack any other seamen who might arrive on their shores and departed for the Hawaiian Islands, then known as the Sandwich Islands. Between January and May 1826, the *Dolphin* remained near Honolulu. This major base for whalers and merchant ships can only be described as a "wide open" town, whose general lawlessness was beginning to pose a threat to its continued use as a merchant shipping stopover. On one occasion, the *Dolphin*'s officers suppressed a riot that threatened the missionary headquarters.

Percival also managed to establish good relations with King Tamehameha, so he secured for American seamen the same rights as British sailors, who had been frequenting the islands for a longer time. Percival aided shipping around the islands and finally returned to Callao. By then, however, he had managed to fall foul of missionary interests, and he finally demanded a court martial, which cleared his name of the complaints laid against him by the missionaries.

A similar cruise was undertaken in 1826 by Captain Thomas Catesby Jones's sloop *Peacock*. She sailed to the Galapagos, Marquesas, Tahiti, and Hawaiian islands before returning to Peru, and Jones helped improve the lot of merchant sailors in Tahiti and Hawaii.

A Voyage to the Antarctic

Other voyages of exploration and diplomacy were made in the Pacific, along the eastern coast of Asia, and in the Indian Ocean as far west as Zanzibar. A purely exploratory and scientific expedition to Antarctica was led by Lieutenant Charles Wilkes with the sloops *Vincennes* and *Peacock*, the brig *Porpoise*, the schooners *Sea Gull* and *Flying Fish*, and the store ship *Relief*. The expedition sailed from Hampton Roads in August 1838, via Madeira, Rio de Janeiro, Cape Horn, Callao, the Tuamotu Islands, and the Society Islands, to Sydney in Australia. From Sydney, an exploration of Antarctica began in January and February 1840. The expedition then visited New Zealand and the Fiji Islands, and reached Honolulu in October 1840. It undertook more surveys south of Hawaii before sailing to the northwestern United States in April 1841. The coasts of Washington, Oregon, and northern California were surveyed before Wilkes's expedition arrived in San Francisco (then called Yuerba Buena) in October 1841. The *Sea Gull* had disappeared without trace in the far south, and the subsequent loss of the *Peacock* off the American coast persuaded Wilkes not to visit Japan as he had planned, but to return home via the

The sloop *Vincennes*, commanded by Lieutenant Charles Wilkes, in Disappointment Bay on January 25, 1840. The bay was named by Wilkes when an ice shelf barred his approach to Antarctica. Wilkes's U.S. Exploring Expedition had discovered the icy continent on January 19, just one day before the arrival of a French expedition 400 miles to the west.

Lieutenant Matthew Fontaine Maury could not undertake sea duty as a result of a leg injury, but on June 29, 1842, he was appointed Superintendent of the Depot of Charts and Instruments. He was a superb choice, for his promotion of research and data collection laid the foundations for the U.S. Navy's later preeminence in oceanography.

islands of the Caroline and East Indies groups, Singapore, Cape Town, and Brazil. He finally returned to New York in June 1842 after nearly four years.

Operations Closer to Home

During this period, the navy had undertaken small-scale operations in home waters as part of the wars with the Seminole and Creek tribes in Florida, Georgia, and Alabama between 1836 and 1842. This work in the confined coastal waters, rivers, and swamps of the region involved the *Constellation*, *St. Louis*, *Concord*, *Vandalia*, *Warren*, and other ships of Commodore Dallas's squadron. The nature of the campaign offered little scope for the use of the larger ships, so the navy's involvement took the form of boat expeditions and shore parties that were often detached from their parent vessels for up to a year.

Perhaps the most interesting of these detachments was Lieutenant Commander J.T. McLaughlin's "mosquito fleet," which operated against the Seminoles who had taken refuge in the Everglades. The "mosquito fleet" was active between 1838 and 1842 from a base at Indian Key on the south coast of Florida. It operated a total of 12 small sailing vessels, two

barges, and 140 canoes, manned by a strength that increased from 160 in 1838 to 622, including 130 marines, during 1842.

The Opening of China

During the 1st Opium War (1839-1842) between the United Kingdom and China, the United States became increasingly worried for the safety of American interests in and around Canton. As a result, Commodore Lawrence Kearney was sent out with a squadron that comprised the *Constellation* and *Boston*. The Americans reached Macao in March 1842 and found the war effectively over. However, Kearney also found the Chinese so disillusioned with the British that they were prepared to deal with the United States on very favorable terms. The Treaty of Nanking ended the 1st Opium War on terms that were commercially very advantageous to the British. Kearney sent three copies of the treaty to the United States, each by a different route to guarantee that at least one reached Washington, and he remained in Canton to negotiate similar benefits for U.S. trade. Kearney eventually left for home after the Chinese had assured him that American interests would receive particular attention.

On his way home, Kearney called at Honolulu and learned that King Tamehameha III had ceded the Hawaiian Islands to the British. Kearney protested so strongly that the king revoked the arrangement.

Three months after Kearney's departure, the Chinese issued a proclamation granting to all nations the rights already granted to the British. The United States wished to validate these rights, and Caleb Cushing was appointed to negotiate a formal treaty. Cushing sailed in the steam frigate *Missouri*, but she was lost in a fire. He finally arrived in China with Commodore Foxhall A. Parker's squadron, which included the frigate *Brandywine*, the sloop *St. Louis*, and the brig *Perry*. A treaty completed in 1844 was later ratified by Congress. Exchange of the ratified documents was entrusted to Alexander

H. Everett, who was to become Commissioner to China. Everett sailed from New York in the ship of the line *Columbus*, accompanied by the sloop *Vincennes* as Commodore James Biddle's squadron. En route to China, Everett became ill, and Biddle assumed his tasks of exchanging the ratified documents and opening a United States legation in Canton.

In 1846 Biddle sailed for home. The squadron's first port of call, Yedo in Japan, was the first time that American ships had dropped anchor in this forbidden kingdom. Biddle managed to communicate with the emperor by an exchange of notes, but failed to secure any rights for U.S. trade. The episode was not completely barren, however, for Biddle gained an insight into the Japanese way of thinking that was to prove very useful eight years later.

The Mexican War

While these events were furthering American trade in the Pacific, events closer to home were drawing the United States toward conflict with Mexico over Texas. The Mexican War, which broke out in 1846, involved two naval squadrons. On the east coast was the Gulf Squadron under Commodore David Conner. Based at Pensacola, Florida, it included the frigate *Potomac*, the sloops *John Adams*, *Falmouth*, *Saratoga*, and *St. Mary's*, the steamers *Mississippi* and *Princeton*, and the brigs *Porpoise*, *Lawrence*, and *Somers*.

The squadron was employed mainly in a conventional role, escorting and supporting the army in its operations on the eastern side of Mexico. Conner's ships also blockaded Mexican east-coast ports and even captured a few of them. On August 7, 1846, Conner tried to capture Alvarado, a small river port 30 miles south of Vera Cruz, where some Mexican gunboats had taken shelter. The attack had to be abandoned because the steam vessels, towing the boats with the landing parties, could make no headway against the current. Another effort was made on October 15, but it too was abandoned after the steam-powered revenue cutter *McLane* ran aground on a sandbar.

The next day, Commodore M.C. Perry, second in command of the Gulf Squadron, left the Vera Cruz area at the head of an expedition to take or destroy Mexican ships sheltering in the Tabasco River on the Yucatan peninsula. Perry's force included the steam frigate *Mississippi*, the small steamers *McLane*, *Vixen*, and *Petrita*, and four other vessels. The force arrived at the mouth of the river on October 23, and took the town of Frontera and several ships in a surprise attack. The smaller vessels then moved 74 miles up the river to Tabasco, where all the Mexican ships present were seized. Perry's force then returned to anchorage off Anton Lizardo, 13 miles south of Vera Cruz, where a floating base had been developed around a supply ship.

Further operations were hampered by supply shortages, but Conner then took virtually his complete strength north to Tampico. A 300-man landing party took

The landing of General Winfield Scott's army near Vera Cruz March 9, 1847. Some 8,600 men were landed without loss at Collado Beach, about 2½ miles south of the Mexican city, in just under five hours by boats from Commodore David Conner's Home Squadron.

Above: U.S. steamers *Scorpion, Spitfire, Vixen,* and *Scourge* with barges full of men, crossing the bar at the mouth of the Tabasco River, June 14, 1847.

Right: Robert F. Stockton was a powerful figure in the development of the U.S. Navy in the "age of sail."

the city without opposition on November 14, capturing three Mexican gunboats and two merchant ships. The Mexicans had withdrawn most of their cannon to Panuco, 80 miles up the river of the same name, but Commander Josiah Tattnall followed with the *Spitfire* and *Petrel*, and on November 19, he landed a party that spiked nine of the guns and destroyed a considerable quantity of supplies.

In December, Perry's force of the *Mississippi, Vixen, Bonita,* and *Petrel*, sailed to Laguna. They occupied the town without opposition, because the local people were not in favor of the Mexican central government. Weather conditions now put the end to all but blockading operations until the spring of 1847. During the winter, the overall plan for U.S. operations in 1847 was changed. The capture of Mexico City was still the object, but the launching point was switched from Monterrey to Vera Cruz. Just before the capture of this important city was attempted, Perry replaced Conner as commander of the Gulf Squadron. Perry was par-

Below: Stockton's squadron off La Paz on the west coast of Mexico. Stockton assumed command of the U.S. naval forces in the Pacific early in the Mexican War and undertook a blockade of the Mexican coast. Combining his effort with those of John C. Fremont and Stephen W. Kearny, Stockton also played a major part in the capture of California for the United States.

ticularly important in the capture of Vera Cruz, for he landed six large naval guns to boost the army artillery engaged in breaching the city's walls from the inland side, and he created a flotilla under Commander Tattnall to destroy the shore end of the city's wall. This flotilla included the *Spitfire*, *Vixen*, *Bonita*, *Reefer*, *Petrel*, *Falcon*, and *Tampico*, all small vessels that had been equipped with at least one heavy, long-range gun.

After a five-day bombardment, Vera Cruz surrendered on March 27, 1847, and the city was developed as the main supply base for the overland advance on Mexico City. Perry also extended U.S. control of Mexico's eastern coast by capturing several other ports, including Alvarado, Tuxpan, Frontera, and Tabasco, which virtually ended the task of the Gulf Squadron in the conflict.

The Capture of California

The Pacific Squadron, based at Callao under Commodore J.D. Sloat, included the *Savannah*, *Levant*, and *Portsmouth*, soon reinforced by the *Cyane*, *Warren*, *Portsmouth*, and supply ship *Erie*. In preparation for war, Sloat was ordered to concentrate his ships in Mexican west-coast ports that were to be taken as soon as hostilities broke out, and then to make the capture of San Francisco his main objective.

Sloat concentrated his squadron at Mazatlan from October 1845, and in March 1846, he sent the *Cyane*, *Warren*, *Portsmouth*, and *Erie* north to California while he remained at Mazatlan with the *Savannah*. Sloat received definite news of the outbreak of war only on June 6, 1846, more than three weeks after the declaration of war. He set sail for Monterey in California, where he joined forces with the *Cyane* and *Levant* on July 2. Here the commodore learned of the uprising of American residents of California, who had declared the Republic of California.

On July 7, Sloat landed 250 sailors and marines, and took possession of Monterey. Two days later, Commander Montgomery of the *Portsmouth* occupied San Francisco. On July 15, Sloat turned over command to Commodore Stockton, who had arrived from the east coast in the frigate *Congress*, and soon returned home in the *Levant*. Stockton continued the task already started by Sloat, resulting in the capture of San Diego, Santa Barbara, San Pedro, and Los Angeles on July 29, August 4, August 6, and August 13 respectively.

Stockton then pulled out most of his southern California garrisons and sailed for San Francisco after hearing reports of a Mexican attack on Sutter's Fort in the Sacramento valley, northeast of San Francisco. This move persuaded some of the Mexicans in southern California to break their parole, and on September 23, they attacked Los Angeles, which was held by Lieutenant Gillespie with just 48 men. Gillespie withstood a siege by 600 men until September 30, when he secured terms for a withdrawal to San Pedro.

A flogging on board the *Cyane* during 1842. Such punishment raised very strong emotions. It was formally abolished by Congress on September 2, 1850.

Shortly afterward, the *Savannah* arrived, and Captain Mervine tried without success to recapture Los Angeles with the help of Gillespie's small force. Stockton had meanwhile discovered that the reports of Mexican activities in central California had been greatly exaggerated, and he hastened to shift the main weight of both naval and land forces back toward southern California. It was only on December 12 that combined army and naval forces recaptured San Diego.

The Mexican resistance was finally broken by the 600-man army and navy force under Stockton's command in the Battle of San Gabriel, about 12 miles from San Francisco, on January 9, 1847. Another U.S. victory followed at La Mesa, and in January 12, the Treaty of Cahuenga yielded California to the United States after a fascinating campaign in which the navy had played the decisive part.

More ships were arriving in the theater, including the *Columbus* on her way home from Japan with Commodore Biddle, and the 54-gun *Independence* from the east coast with Commodore Shubrick. Biddle was the senior officer and assumed overall command. Shubrick was sent with the *Independence* and *Cyane* to join the *Portsmouth* in the blockade of Mazatlan and Guaymas, and these three ships were later reinforced by the *Erie*, Biddle then turned command of the Pacific Squadron over to Shubrick and returned home.

On October 19, Captain Lavalette of the *Congress* demanded the surrender of Guaymas and, after the withdrawal of the Mexican garrison, occupied the port. The Mexicans tried to recapture Guaymas several weeks later, but were driven back by a naval garrison under Commander Selfridge.

On November 11, Shubrick arrived off Mazatlan with the *Independence, Congress, Cyane,* and *Erie.* Some 730 men were landed, found no opposition, and seized Mazatlan. The Mexicans had retreated about ten miles to Urias, where they were routed on November 20 by a combined land and water attack under Lavalette. San Blas was occupied without opposition on January 12, 1848, by a party from Captain T. Bailey's *Lexington.*

This marked the official end of operations before the Mexican surrender in the Treaty of Guadalupe Hidalgo on February 2, but small-scale actions continued before news of the treaty reached outlying areas. The most notable was at San Jose in southern California. Arriving on February 14, Commander S.F. DuPont of the *Cyane* found the place held by Mexicans and Indians, who were besieging a U.S. force in a mission about three miles away. Commanded by Lieutenant Heywood, the 25-man garrison had held

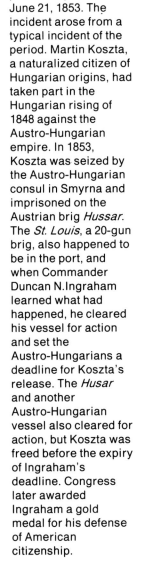

The *St. Louis* (left) and *Hussar* at the Turkish port of Smyrna on June 21, 1853. The incident arose from a typical incident of the period. Martin Koszta, a naturalized citizen of Hungarian origins, had taken part in the Hungarian rising of 1848 against the Austro-Hungarian empire. In 1853, Koszta was seized by the Austro-Hungarian consul in Smyrna and imprisoned on the Austrian brig *Hussar*. The *St. Louis*, a 20-gun brig, also happened to be in the port, and when Commander Duncan N.Ingraham learned what had happened, he cleared his vessel for action and set the Austro-Hungarians a deadline for Koszta's release. The *Husar* and another Austro-Hungarian vessel also cleared for action, but Koszta was freed before the expiry of Ingraham's deadline. Congress later awarded Ingraham a gold medal for his defense of American citizenship.

out despite several attacks, low provisions, and sickness. DuPont landed a force that drove out the Mexicans and Indians.

Still Greater Prosperity

Despite the war with Mexico, this was the beginning of a period of rapidly increasing prosperity for the United States. Between 1846 and the beginning of the Civil War in 1861, U.S. foreign trade more than trebled in value from $235 million to $762 million, and almost two-thirds of this trade was carried by American merchant shipping. Most of this trade was with European countries, especially the United Kingdom, but Asian countries gradually assumed a more important position as American traders exploited the opportunities already opened by China and soon to be opened by Japan.

In April 1849, Commander James Glynn's 16-gun sloop *Preble* arrived from Hong Kong in the Japanese port of Nagasaki. Operating under the orders of Commodore David Geisinger, Glynn was charged with securing the release of 15 sailors from the whaler *Lagoda*. Using a combination of common sense, severity, and self assurance, Glynn succeeded in his mission and came away with further clues about the best methods of negotiating with the Japanese.

The Opening of Japan

The breakthrough in negotiations with Japan was achieved by Commodore M.C. Perry, who arrived in Hong Kong in April 1853 and then moved toward Japan via the Ryukyu and Bonin islands, where he secured the support of the local populations and bases from which to approach Japan. On July 8, 1853, Perry anchored in Yedo Bay with his flagship, the *Susquehanna*, the frigate *Mississippi*, and the sloops *Saratoga* and *Plymouth*. Initial negotiations were completed with imperial government officials, and Perry left for Hong Kong in July.

In February 1854, Perry returned to Yedo Bay with a squadron that included the steamships *Susquehanna, Mississippi*, and *Powhatan*, and the sailing vessels *Macedonian, Vandalia, Southampton*, and *Lexington*. The squadron later moved to Yokohama Bay, and a protracted but friendly bout of negotiations ended with the signature on March 31 of a treaty that opened the ports of Hakodadi and Shimoda to American ships. It was a considerable breakthrough, and soon American trade with Japan was growing rapidly.

Throughout the rest of the 1850s, the navy continued with the same basic tasks that it had undertaken between the end of the War of 1812 and the outbreak of the Mexican War, aiding U.S. trade all over the world, surveying, and honing seafaring skills.

Commodore Perry lands at Yokohama to meet the Japanese commissioners on March 8, 1854. This started the process of negotiation that resulted in the Treaty of Kanagawa on March 31, promising peace and friendship between the United States and the Japanese empire.

U.S. ARMY UNIFORMS (1775-1939)

Infantry

The first North American soldiers to don any type of uniform were the members of the militia units raised by individual governors and towns in the period before the Revolutionary War. At the beginning of the Revolution, these men fought in their original uniforms, which for obvious reasons were similar in concept (if not detail design) to British uniforms. The fledgling United States lacked any means to manufacture a standardized uniform for its troops, who therefore had to go to war in their civilian clothes. In this event, trappers and hunters were better off than their urban counterparts. Their normal clothes were well suited to outdoor life. They had a certain natural camouflage factor, as well as being durable and comfortable.

The number and diversity of the uniforms worn by the militia units were enormous, so the few examples here illustrate just a few of the better-known outfits. In the Battalion of Independent Foot Companies of Militia, New York City, the grenadier company wore a blue uniform with red distinctions, the fusilier company a blue uniform with red distinctions and a fur cap carrying the legend "*Fusiliers - salus populi suprema lex,*" and the German fusilier company a blue uniform with red distinctions, silver lace, and the legend "German Fusiliers" on the cap plate. The Union, Light Infantry, and Oswego Rangers also wore a blue uniform with red distinctions and white undergarments (waistcoat and breeches). The Bold Foresters wore a green coat and a round hat which turned up at the sides and had a plate inscribed "Freedom." The Sportsmans Company and the Corsicans and Rangers wore green coats with distinctions of buff and carmine respectively. The New York Independent Companies of Rangers had a blue uniform with white distinctions and a helmet sporting a white-painted skull and crossbones above the word "Liberty."

Other corps uniformed in the European fashion included the Massachusetts and Connecticut militias, which wore red coats. The 1st Company of the Governor's Foot Guards of Connecticut was particularly resplendent in red coats with black lapels, yellow lace and white skirt cuffs, yellow undergarments, and red-plumed fur caps. The 2nd Company had red coats with buff distinctions and white metal buttons, and white undergarments. Another notable outfit was the Light Company of the 1st Philadelphia Battalion, which wore light blue coats with buff distinctions.

Most of the new corps chose a uniform modeled on the dress of hunters and trappers. The Maryland Rifles, for example, wore green hunting shirts, while the men of Morgan's Riflemen, the 1st Virginia Regiment of Infantry, and the 5th Regiment of South Carolina Riflemen all wore white hunting shirts bought at their own expense. General George Washington recommended the hunting shirt to all units that could not get proper uniforms, for it would suggest to the British that every man so attired was an expert marksman.

In 1775, the U.S. units were ordered to adopt a brown uniform with regiments identified by their distinctions. Not all regiments conformed, however, and in 1775 the New York infantry included the 1st Regiment with blue coats and carmine distinctions, the 2nd Regiment with light brown coats and blue distinctions, the 3rd Regiment with gray coats and green distinctions, and the 4th Regiment with dark brown coats and scarlet distinctions. In Connecticut, the pre-war red coat was retained. In Pennsylvania, the 1st Regiment wore brown coats with buff distinctions, the 2nd Regiment blue coats with red distinctions as well as round black hats. The 3rd Regiment wore brown coats with white distinctions as well as tricorn hats with white lace, the 4th and 5th Regiments blue coats with white distinctions, and the 6th Regiment blue coats with red distinctions. In New Jersey, blue uniforms were the most common, but some units wore red coats with white distinctions.

So varied were these and other uniforms that recognition of an American soldier was virtually impossible. In 1777, therefore, it was ordered that all U.S. soldiers should wear a sprig of green in the hat as an identifying mark.

Officers frequently wore a coat different in color and style from that of their men. During 1777, the great administrator and trainer von Steuben noted uniforms as varied as blue coats with white distinctions, red with black, brown with sea green, lined white with silver lace, and gray with buff. Some of the least showy of the American units were the Pennsylvania regiments, whose plain yellowish-brown coats resulted in the nickname the "Quaker Brigade."

In October 1779, a contemporary record indicates that the New Hampshire, Massachusetts, Rhode Island, and Connecticut regiments wore blue coats with white distinctions, that the New York and New Jersey regiments wore blue and buff coats with white skirt turnbacks and white undergarments, that the Pennsylvania, Delaware, Maryland, and Virginia regiments wore blue coats with red distinctions, and that the North Carolina, South Carolina, and Georgia regiments wore blue coats with white distinctions. From the same time, a black and white cockade became standard, the white symbolic of France, whose support was so vital to the eventual American success in the war.

Bandsmen generally wore a version of the regimental uniform with the colors reversed; another notable exception to the groupings mentioned above was the Commander-in-Chief's Guard, whose members wore a blue coat with white distinctions, white undergarments, black half-gaiters, and a hat with a blue and white feather.

In 1782, it was ordered that all cavalry

By the time of the Battle of Gettysburg in July 1863, most of the Federal army had been kitted out in the blue uniform that had been standardized in 1862 and universally adopted by late 1863.

This fine photographic study of General Hugh Judsen "Kill Cavalry" Kilpatrick shows the uniform typically worn by general officers.

and infantry regiments should wear blue uniforms with red distinctions, white linings, and white metal buttons. The state of the country and the treasury meant that it was 1796 before this order had been fully implemented. The comparable bandsman's uniform included a red coat with blue distinctions and undergarments. In 1797, the black and white cockade was replaced by a black cockade with a white eagle on it.

The cocked hat was abolished in 1802, when it was replaced by a crested helmet, and it was also ordered that blue pants should be worn in winter and white ones during the summer.

Further change came in 1808, when the original long coat was supplanted by a single-breasted coatee adorned down the front by silver lace loops. The headdress that went with it was a cylindrical hat with a cockade and plume on its left side. Noncommissioned officers were distinguishable by a yellow epaulet, worn on the right shoulder by sergeants and the left shoulder by corporals. The red distinctions were ordered out of existence in 1812, and the blue jacket was fastened by ten white metal buttons with black twisted loops. The blue collar was edged in white, fastened by two buttons and narrow white lace loops, while the blue cuffs had three white metal buttons with black loops. The headdress was a shako, with a yellow metal plate carrying an eagle motif, a white plume and white cords.

Although a standard Federal uniform was available during the second half of the Civil War, there was an amazing variety in the combinations that could be worn in individual personal style.

As was common in armies of the day, riflemen wore a uniform different from that of line infantrymen. A U.S. rifleman wore an all-gray uniform with a looped front, with buttons located at the apex of the ''Vs'' thus formed. Similar loops and three buttons featured on the cuffs, with the buttons laid out one above the other. The collar was similar to that of the infantrymen, but was gray with black loops and lace. The buttons were of yellow metal. The leather equipment and headdress of the rifleman was similar to those of the infantryman in basic design. The leather was white, and the shako had a badge of yellow metal shaped like a hunting horn, and a green plume and cords. The officers of both infantry and rifle regiments wore long-skirted coatees and tall bicorner hats.

In 1821, the United States declared blue the national color. In the resulting redesign of the standard uniform, considerable efforts were made to simplify its manufacture and wearability. Red coats were reserved for bandsmen, and the rank distinctions of noncommissioned officers were moved on the sleeves.

In 1835, the shako was modified. The original pattern, in which there was considerable outward curve toward the crown, was replaced by a more straight-sided design, and the cords were removed. The shako's badge was also modified to a white metal eagle over a hunting horn. The blue shoulder straps were replaced by white epaulets, and the cuffs were also made white. The loops on the front of the coat were abolished, and a gray-blue color was standardized for the pants. A more unusual feature was the matching cuff patches. There were no cuffs as such, and the patches had white piping on three sides, together with two buttons and loops. The distinctive service uniform of the period consisted of gray-blue pants and a shell jacket, without cuffs but with two buttons on the lower seam. Worn with this service uniform was a soft blue forage cap.

A completely new uniform was introduced in 1851. The new pattern included a dark blue tunic without any piping. The collar was light blue and carried the regimental number in yellow at its ends, the cuffs were light blue and pointed, and the epaulets were light blue. The pants were unaltered apart from the introduction of a light blue stripe along each outside leg seam. The shako gave way to a tall, dark blue kepi with a light blue pompom and light blue band. All leather equipment now became black. Officers had neither colored distinctions nor lapels, and in undress and off-duty wore passants on their shoulders.

The passant was a rectangle of cloth, lace or lace-edged, worn at the point of the shoulder parallel to the sleeve seam. It carried the officer's rank insignia: nothing for a 2nd lieutenant, one gold bar for a 1st lieutenant, two gold bars for a captain, one gold leaf for a major, one silver leaf for a lieutenant colonel, and one silver eagle for a colonel. These insignia were repeated on the straps of the epaulets. The raised, oval cloth crescent on the epaulet also carried the regimental number in yellow, and the number was repeated, together with a bugle motif, on the band of the kepi.

The men retained the earlier undress jacket, and later changes included the the abolition of epaulets and bandsman's lapels in 1855, the replacement of the kepi's colored band by colored piping, and the abolition of the bandsman's red coats in 1857.

In 1861, the collar and cuffs were changed to dark blue with light blue piping, and yellow metal shoulder scales were introduced. At the same time, full-dress pants were altered to dark blue, and the tall kepi was abolished in favor of a black lacquered hat with a turned-up left side, regimental number, and a black feather. Service dress included a low kepi of dark blue, a short-skirted jacket also of dark blue with a turn-down collar of the same color and no colored distinctions, and the old gray-blue pants without piping. This was the standard uniform of the Union soldier in the Civil War.

The outbreak of the Civil War meant that many militia units, with their ex-travagant and brightly colored uniforms, were called out. The 79th Regiment of New York Militia, for example, wore Scottish highland dress. Many units wore the 1851 pattern tall kepi, together with double-breasted coats and epaulets; typical of this group was the 2nd Regiment of the New York Militia. One Ohio regiment wore short open jackets, and another very popular uniform type was that of the Zouaves. In their original French form, these units were light infantry raised from the population of France's North African empire, who were notable for their superb drill and fascinating blend of local dress adapted to European concepts. Many units called into Union service wore Zouave uniform; notable examples were the 5th New York ("Duryee Zouaves") and the 11th New York ("1st New York Fire Zouaves" and "Ellsworth's Zouaves"). Though each of these Zouave units wore the same basic pattern of uniform, there were enormous differences in detail and color. The pants were generally blue or red, and were mainly of the baggy North African cut, although long pants were also worn. The distinctive jacket came in a bewildering assortment of styles and colors, and the headdress was a fez or kepi. There was also a strong Italian influence in the some militia units. The Fire Zouaves wore a Garibaldi shirt for a time, while the Garibaldi Guard wore the Italian *Bersaglieri* uniform.

On the other side of the front line, the Confederate troops wore a service uniform consisting of a broad-brimmed gray hat or a gray kepi with a blue band, a short blue-gray jacket without any colored distinctions but with pointed cuffs carrying black piping and yellow metal buttons, and brown leather equipment. The everyday uniform consisted of a double-breasted gray coat with a blue collar, piping, and pointed cuffs, together with the standard blue-gray pants and kepi; the equipment was black leather. There were many non-standard Confederate volunteer units, and many frequently adopted the Zouave uniform and other outlandish kit. As the war swung decisively against the Confederacy, the troops found it increasingly difficult to get uniforms, and many units ended the war with a hodgepodge of uniform and civilian clothing. At the end of the war, Confederate uniforms were abandoned.

The pattern of the standard infantry uniform was altered again in 1872. A new tunic introduced shorter skirts, white collar patches for the regimental number, white shoulder straps, and white double-scalloped cuff patches. The tunic had white piping down the front, and the lace of noncommissioned officers became white. The headdress was a blue cloth-covered shako with white piping, a white pompom in the shape of a fir cone and, in the case of officers, a drooping plume. Officers also wore a blue double-breasted coat, without colored distinctions but with epaulets. The cuffs carried no patches, but did include lace loops, pointed at the top. A gold-laced waist belt replaced the earlier black belt, and the previous crimson sashes were abolished.

The pants were gray with a single, dark blue stripe down the outer seams.

In 1881, a spiked helmet was introduced, together with an all-white tunic collar on which the previous regimental numbers were abolished, as was the pouch belt that had been worn over the shoulder. Bandsmen were indentifiable by the white lace loops on the front of their tunics, and the paired white stripes on their pants. The officer's uniform remained basically unchanged, but was augmented by a blue single-breasted jacket with passants and breast and skirt pockets. In 1896, a buttonless jacket with broad lace on the collar, down the front, around the hem, and on the hip vents appeared.

From 1888, service dress included gaiters that were laced up the sides. The officer's spiked helmet was distinguishable by the small gold chain that ran from a point high on the right side to low on

This drum band of a Federal regiment illustrates the standardized uniform of the late Civil War.

the left side. Field officers wore a horsehair plume drooping toward the rear, together with a cord in the distinguishing color of their branch of the service. The peaked cap had a low, comparatively small crown.

The jacket worn by enlisted men had altered little since 1861, and with it a gray soft hat indented from front to back was worn, though white cork helmets were worn for tropical service. A khaki uniform was adopted in 1898 after the experience in the Spanish-American War. The jacket had five buttons on the front, and there were patch pockets on the breast and skirts. The usual summer wear was a shirt, that of an officer being distinguishable by its passants.

During 1903, the distinctive color of the infantry reverted to light blue. The collar, shoulder strap, and cuffs were dark blue with light blue piping, and the cuff patches were eliminated. On the full dress

uniform, a plaited cord was attached across the breast. The pants stripes of the enlisted men were removed. The kepi and the spiked helmet were both replaced by a small forage cap with a flat top and two light blue stripes around it. The officer's uniform retained its double-breasted frock coat, but the collar and cap band were light blue with gold lace, and the epaulets were replaced by plaited shoulder cords. The cuffs were gold piped, with a varying number of gold knots to indicate rank. Between the cuff and the knots was the branch-of-service badge.

In 1912, a few small changes were promulgated. The forage cap's crown was widened slightly, and on the felt hat, the front-to-back single indentation was replaced by four dents. The service dress of olive drab was modified very little in World War I.

In this conflict, the only major adoption was the round-crowned steel helmet modeled on that of the British army. Branch of service was indicated by the color of the hat cord (blue for the infantry), and by a bronze button on each collar point: the right button had the initials "ULS" above the designation of the wearer's regiment, and the left button had the branch-of-service badge (crossed rifles for the infantry) above the company initial. On the ends of their collars, officers wore the bronze initials "U.S." above the branch-of-service badge. During World War I, a fore-and-aft cap was adopted. The enlisted man had a badge that marked the wearer's branch of service and was located on the left side of the turn-up, while the officer had piping in branch-of-service color around the turn-up with rank badges on the left side.

The dress uniform was abolished after World War I. The service dress was revised in 1926 to include an open-necked jacket together with buttons and insignia of gilt metal rather than bronze. The branch-of-service and national initials were located on the lapels. Equipment was brown leather for officers and gray-green webbing for enlisted men. The uniform was the same basic stye for all branches of the army. Officers sported a dark brown cloth stripe of medium width around the cuff. On the peaked forage cap, officers wore the national eagle, and enlisted men their branch-of-service badge.

Cavalry

During the Revolutionary War, American cavalrymen equaled their infantry counterparts in the wide assortment of their uniforms. To give just a few examples, the City of Philadelphia Cavalry during 1775 wore a brown coat with white distinctions, and a black helmet; Lee's Cavalry used a blue coat with white distinctions, a white vest, and black breeches; in 1776, part of the 1st Continental Regiment of Light Dragoons had a blue coat with red distinctions, while the rest of the men wore a brown coat with green distinctions; in 1780, the 4th Continental Regiment of Light Dragoons had a red coat, and later a green coat with red lapels; Washington's Mounted Lifeguard sported a white uniform with light blue collars, lapels, cuffs, skirts, and vest, together with a leather helmet carrying a fox-

tail; and Colonel Marion's Cavalry (South Carolina) had a leather helmet carrying a white metal scroll emblazoned with the legend ''Death or Liberty.''

During 1779, the light dragoons had a blue coat with white distinctions, changed in 1800 to a green coat with black collars, lapels, and cuffs together with white linings and undergarments, yellow metal shoulder scales and buttons, and yellow button loops. The leather helmet had a black horsehair mane with a yellow metal plate on the front, while the officers also wore a green plume.

Between 1802 and 1810, the cavalry wore the infantry uniform, but by 1812 its regiments had a white skirt turnback. In 1814, the dragoons were distinguished by orange piping and lace loops, while the other regiments had yellow piping and lace loops. The uniform then underwent the same changes as the infantry in the period up to the outbreak of the Civil War, though the branch-of-service color was yellow rather than blue. The same color was then worn by Confederate cavalry in the Civil War with the same basic uniform as the infantry. Another change in the

The Battle of Cedar Creek in October 1864 was one of the high points of General Philip Sheridan's Shenandoah Valley campaign. By this late stage in the Civil War, the Federal army was well equipped and fully kitted out in a standard uniform, whereas the Confederate army had been reduced to a miscellany of clothing.

period leading to the Civil War was the adoption of a white plume on the shako during 1835. In 1846, the army raised a regiment of mounted riflemen with a uniform of blue with green piping. In 1861, the cavalry was completely reorganized as the 1st to 6th Cavalry Regiments and adopted a black felt campaign hat with its brim turned up on one side and often adorned with a black ostrich feather. The branch-of-service emblem was a pair of crossed sabers.

The dark blue dress uniform had a short coat piped in yellow on all seams, and the collar was embellished with two yellow button loops and a small button at each end. In the period between 1881 and 1903, the cavalry wore the same tunic as the infantry, though the piping was yellow rather than blue and continued right around the hem, and the skirt pocket flaps were different, with two buttons and made of yellow material. The spiked helmet had yellow lines and a yellow plume falling to the rear.

The Indian Scouts, raised in 1870, wore a version of the standard cavalry uniform with white distinctions and red piping, while the helmet carried a plume of red and white. The branch-of-service badge was a pair of crossed arrows surmounted by the initials "U.S.S." which was retained, together with a white and red hat cord, right into the 1930s.

In 1903, the cavalry adopted the same pattern of uniform as the infantry, distinguishable only by the yellow piping and branch-of-service emblem.

Artillery

The first U.S. artillery units were raised in 1777, and in 1779 the uniform was fixed as a dark blue coat with red collar, lapels, cuffs, and skirt lining, and yellow metal buttons. The lapels, buttonholes, and black tricorn hat were all edged in narrow yellow lace, and the hat had a red feather plume. The breeches and leather equipment were white.

In 1794, the artillery introduced a new headdress in the form of a black leather helmet with a front-to-back black crest

and a red plume on the left side, though the plume color was changed to red and black stripes during 1800. The officers wore gold epaulets. In 1812, the artillery adopted the infantry uniform with yellow piping and buttons, and the shako was modified with a branch-of-service emblem made up of a pair of crossed cannon barrels under the national eagle emblem. In 1835, the branch-of-service color was changed to red, and all piping was therefore switched. The artillery subsequently changed its uniform with the infantry, but retained the distinguishing branch-of-service color. In 1861, the artillery adopted a red horsehair plume on its shako, and in 1881, the horse artillery adopted the same tunic as the cavalry. Thereafter the artillery uniform matched that of the infantry and from 1903 sported the crossed cannon branch-of-service badge.

Corps of Engineers

The uniform of the engineers in general paralleled that of the infantry and artillery. In 1780, the engineers wore a blue coat with buff distinctions and undergarments. These colors were retained until 1821, when engineer officers switched to black velvet collars and cuffs and the distinctive emblem of a star in a laurel wreath. The men wore a blue uniform with yellow piping. In 1853, the distinctive emblem changed to a castle with three towers, and in 1874, the distinctive color was changed to red with white piping. Thereafter, the corps of engineers used the same uniform as the infantry with the exception of its red and white branch-of-service color and distinctive badge.

Signal Corps

Dating from the time of the Civil War, the Signal Corps has always worn the same uniform as the infantry except for its orange and white branch-of-service color and distinctive badge of two crossed signal flags above a flaming torch.

Continued from page 93

Woodrow Wilson
For further references
see pages
123, 124, 130

canal between the Gulf of Mexico and the Pacific Ocean. Congress had already provided the legislative framework for the whole scheme and immediately appropriated the necessary funding as the Isthmian Canal Commission debated the problem of who should build the canal.

The commission reported to President Roosevelt that the task was too great to be entrusted to a private company, and the president then turned the task over to the army. Roosevelt reorganized the commission, adding to it several specialists drawn mainly from the Corps of Engineers. In 1907, Colonel George W. Goethals was appointed as the commission's chairman and chief engineer. An engineer officer since 1882, Goethals had sole administrative responsibility for the vast project, and he proved himself an outstanding organizer before the canal was completed, after problems in engineering, labor relations, housing, and sanitation had been overcome. Another major part in the project's success was played by the army's Medical Department, which successfully entrusted Colonel William G. Gorgas with the tasks of controlling malaria and eliminating yellow fever.

The opening of the Panama Canal in 1914 marked a decisive point in the evolution of the United States' military posture, for the canal allowed rapid movement of even the navy's largest battleships between the Atlantic and Pacific oceans, and therefore removed the need to maintain large standing fleets in each ocean. Such was the importance of the canal, therefore, that its protection immediately became one of the army's greatest priorities. The Panama Canal Zone was henceforward a strategic point in the army's continental defense plans and was protected by modern fortifications occupied by a large garrison.

Trouble in Mexico

The building of the Panama Canal and peace-keeping operations in Central America and the Caribbean were typical of the "hemispheric defense concerns" of the United States during the first years of the 20th century. Altogether closer to home were problems with Mexico, which, after a period of relative stability, entered a tumultuous period in May 1911. The era was sparked by the overthrow of President Porfirio Diaz, who had ruled Mexico since 1877. A bitter civil war between Francisco Madero and Victoriano Huerta followed, resulting in Madero's defeat and death in February 1913. The Huerta regime was challenged by Venustiano Carranza, leader of the Constitutionalist party, and Emiliano Zapata, leader of the rival Radical party.

To protect the southern part of the United States against any overspill from this tangled Mexican situation, President Taft ordered the strengthening of the southern frontier in 1911 by establishing the provisional maneuver division, already mentioned, at San Antonio. Succeeding Taft as president in March 1913, Woodrow Wilson would not concede that Huerta had attained power by legitimate means and refused to recognize his government. Wilson placed an embargo on the delivery of American weapons to either side in the civil war, but when in 1914 Huerta appeared to be gaining a possibly decisive superiority over Carranza, Wilson lifted the embargo on the delivery of arms to the Carranzistas.

The Tampico Incident

Such a move inevitably attracted the anger of the Huertistas and equally inevitably led to an international incident, involving sailors from the despatch boat U.S.S. *Dolphin*, who were sent into Tampico on April 9, 1914, to pick up supplies. As the boat tied up at the dock, Huertista soldiers marched onto it and arrested the sole officer and his enlisted men, who were then marched through the streets of Tampico. The Americans were released almost immediately, and Huerta expressed his regrets about the episode. This was not enough for the commander of the American naval forces in the area, Rear Admiral Henry T. Mayo, who demanded a public apology. Huerta refused, and Wilson saw an opportunity for the intervention which he now regarded as vital to the survival of the Carranzistas. Wilson therefore agreed

Pancho Villa
For further references
see pages
124, *125*,126, *127*

Venustiano Carranza
For further references
see pages
122, 124, 127, 130

with a naval plan to deny Huerta the use of Mexico's two main east coast ports, Tampico and Veracruz.

Veracruz is Seized

Orders for the implementation of the plan were issued on April 20, when the American consul in Veracruz reported that a German ship was due to dock on the following morning with a consignment of weapons for Huerta. At dawn on April 21, parties from several American warships landed and seized the port. Severe fighting broke out, but with the support of naval gunfire, the Americans gained control of the whole city by the evening of April 22. By the end of the month. American forces in Veracruz totaled 8,000 men (half marines and half soldiers) under the command of Major General Funston. Huerta severed relations with the United States, and Carranza was so angry with this insult to Mexican sovereignty that he too threatened to break off relations. However, one of Carranza's military leaders, Pancho Villa, declared that "It is Huerta's bull that is being gored" and persuaded Carranza to let the episode pass. Mediation by South American countries followed, and on November 25, the last American troops were pulled out of Veracruz.

Shot by a Mexican sniper, Private Daniel Aleysius was the first American killed at Veracruz at the start of the troubles with Mexico.

123

The flag-draped coffins of Americans killed at Veracruz on board the battleship U.S.S. *Montana* in July 1914.

The American occupation lasted longer than originally planned because of Carranza's annoyance, but it did have the effect of cutting virtually all of Huerta's revenues from trade. On August 15, 1914, the Carranzistas captured Mexico City, and Huerta followed Diaz into European exile as Carranza became president.

Carranza proved no more capable than Huerta of bringing peace to Mexico. He was suspicious of Villa's ambitions and therefore refused to give this northern Mexican leader a senior position or even to acknowledge the very real part played by his Division of the North in the Carranzista victory. In November 1914, Villa broke with Carranza and started another chapter in the history of the Mexican revolution.

Villa soon had control of most of northern Mexico, and after forming an alliance with Zapata, he captured Mexico City. Carranza re-established his capital at Veracruz and entrusted operations against Villa to General Alvaro Obregon, a capable commander who drove Villa from Mexico City and then pushed him back into northern Mexico in a series of well-planned operations. Despite its precarious nature, the Carranzista government was recognized by the United States on October 9, 1915.

Villa was based in Chihuahua state, where his forces were reorganizing and building up their strength for the capture of a Carranzista stronghold in Villista territory. This was Agua Prieta, in the neighboring state of Sonora just across the border from Douglas, Arizona.

Agua Prieta could not be reinforced by the Carranzistas via any Mexican route, so Wilson allowed several trains carrying men, weapons, and other supplies to reach Agua Prieta through the United States. Villa learned not only of the United States' recognition of Carranza, but also of its active support for his government, as his army descended from the mountains on October 30. Villa was furious.

The United States Falls Foul of Villa's Anger

Villa attacked on November 1 in the dashing style that had won him several victories in earlier campaigns. Here it resulted in total disaster, for Agua Prieta had been turned into a veritable fortress with entrenchments, barbed wire entanglements, and a plentiful supply of ammunition for both light and heavy weapons. Worse was to follow, for when Villa bypassed Agua Prieta to move on Hermosillo, the capital of Sonora state, his army was cut to pieces when it launched an unprepared daylight attack against a well-prepared and well-armed enemy.

The remnants of Villa's army streamed north toward Nogales, a border town held by Villista guerrillas. The move soon turned into a disorganized rout, and as they looted and murdered their way north, the Villistas blamed their defeat on the United States. Arriving in Nogales, these 300 or 400 survivors fired into the United States, but were soon deterred by the accuracy and volume of the returned

fire. Villa and his men then disappeared into the mountains once more.

Several weeks passed in which nothing was heard of Villa, and Carranza informed the United States that the problem was at an end. That Villa had not been finished was soon revealed afterwards, however, when several American mining engineers were massacred. They were dragged off a train at Santa Ysabel in Chihuahua and shot down by a Villista gang led by Colonel Pablo Lopez. One man pretended to be dead and escaped to reveal what had happened.

Villa Attacks Columbus, New Mexico

Wilson refused to consider military action against Villa, but then Villa once more revealed his presence in February 1916 as he began to move north with about 400 men. Rumor suggested that Villa intended to seek refuge in the United States, but the truth was very different. On March 9, 1916, the Villistas burst into Columbus, New Mexico, and neighboring Camp Fur-

Pancho Villa rides alongside part of his "army" that proved such a troublesome thorn in the side of the United States.

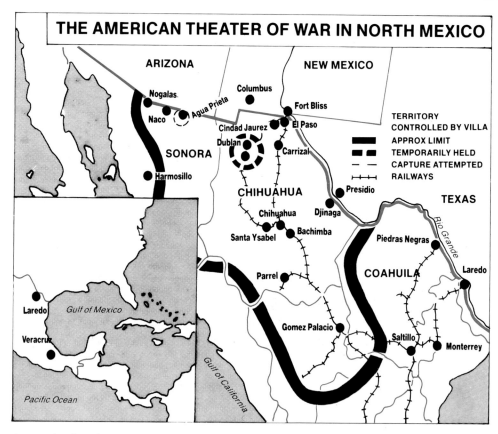

THE AMERICAN THEATER OF WAR IN NORTH MEXICO

long, the headquarters and other main base of Colonel Herbert Slocum's 13th Cavalry Regiment, which was taken by surprise but then responded with commendable speed. The fighting lasted for about three hours before the Villistas were driven back with the loss of about 100 men. A hot pursuit was rapidly organized by a 13th Cavalry detachment under Major Frank Tomkins. He followed the Villistas deep into Mexico, finally caught up with them, and then inflicted heavy losses on them.

In Columbus, 14 soldiers and ten civilians had been killed, which infuriated public and political feelings alike. Wilson immediately ordered the strengthening of the border to prevent any repetition of the event, and this effort eventually soaked up 158,000 men of the regular army and National Guard, most of the United States' active military strength at the time.

Pershing's Punitive Expedition

At the same time, Brigadier General John J. Pershing was ordered to take the field against Villa in Mexico. The American press reported that Pershing's orders were to take Villa "dead or alive," but in fact the commander's instructions were to disperse and if possible to destroy the Villista bands that had invaded the United States. Formally called the Punitive Expedition, Pershing's force had about 10,000 men of two infantry regiments, several cavalry regiments, several batteries of light artillery, support elements and, as a complete novelty in American military operations, the fixed-wing aircraft of the 1st Aero Squadron.

The Punitive Expedition crossed into Mexico on March 15, 1916. Pershing and the administration believed that the expedition would receive at least the tacit support of the Carranzista government, but this renewed infringement of Mexican sovereignty was received with a hostility that was passive only at first.

It is often thought that the Punitive Expedition was a failure because it did not capture Villa. The truth is rather different, for in a period of several weeks, the expedition effectively ended the threat posed by Villa. This success was achieved by small detachments of American cavalry, which moved swiftly

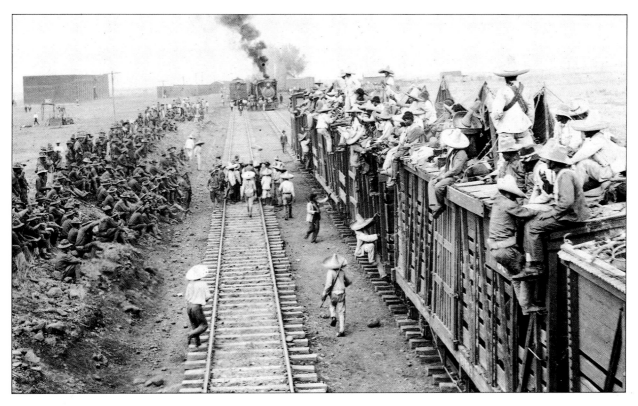

U.S. troops search a train in northern Mexico for evidence of Pancho Villa and his men.

over considerable distances to surprise and defeat the various Villista bands, often killing their leaders and thereby severing the command link between Villa and his men.

As this program was bearing its fruit, the passive reluctance of the Carranzista government was turning to open hostility. Carranza placed such restrictions on American use of the Mexican railroads that supply by this means became impossible. The Americans therefore had to use local sources of supply, which in April led to the first example of open hostility. A squadron of the 13th Cavalry entered Parral to buy supplies and was attacked by a Mexican mob urged on by a German woman, the wife of a Villista. The commander managed to extricate his squadron without loss on either side, but as it pulled back from Parral, the American unit was attacked by men of the Carranzista garrison. While they had been able to avoid using their weapons in the town, here the Americans had no choice and inflicted such losses on the Carranzistas that they broke off the attack.

On June 16, Pershing received a message from the Carranzista commander in Chihuahua state, General Jacinto Trevino,

that the only direction the Americans were now permitted to move was north, back to the United States. Movement in any other direction, Trevino added, would be forcefully resisted. Pershing replied that he was prepared to take orders only from his own government.

The "Battle of Carrizal"

The result was an engagement at Carrizal on June 21, 1916. Part of the 10th Cavalry Regiment collided with Mexican regular forces in a short but very sharp action. The American strength was three officers, two civilian guides, and 79 cavalrymen, and they suffered an undoubted tactical defeat at the hands of the much larger Mexican force. Two of the officers were killed early in the fight and the third was wounded, while most of the non-commissioned officers were also killed or wounded. The Carranzistas did cut off and capture some of the cavalrymen, but most of the Americans managed to fight their way out of the encirclement. It was a hollow victory for the Carranzistas, however, for their admitted losses, including General Felix Gomez killed in the first

A Martin pusher **biplane is of great** historical importance as one of the first aircraft used specifically for bombing. The type was fitted under the lower wing with a rack for three bombs, and successful trials helped to confirm that bombing was indeed a practical method of attacking the enemy.

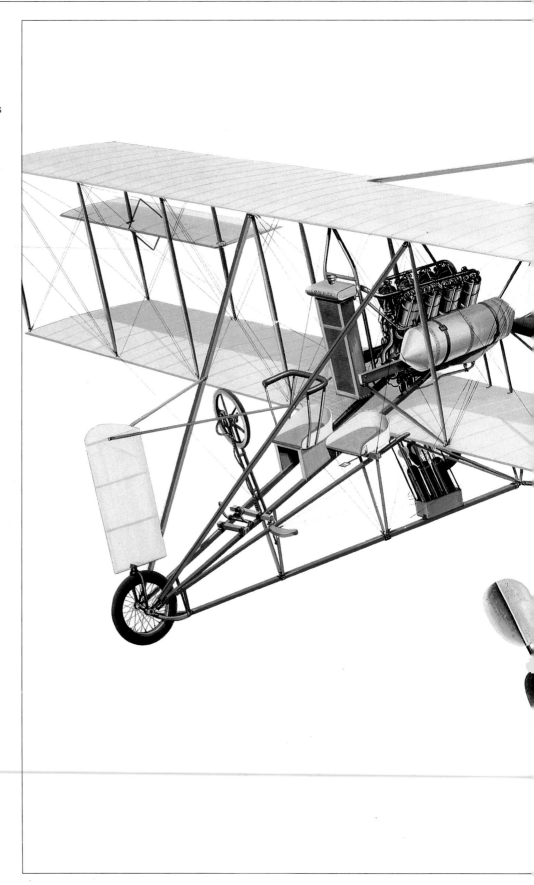

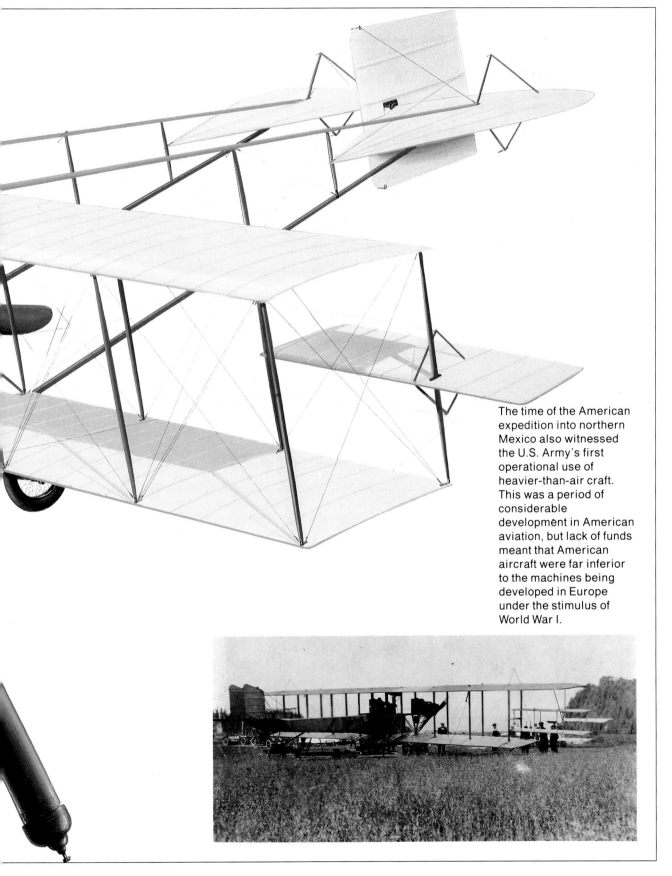

The time of the American expedition into northern Mexico also witnessed the U.S. Army's first operational use of heavier-than-air craft. This was a period of considerable development in American aviation, but lack of funds meant that American aircraft were far inferior to the machines being developed in Europe under the stimulus of World War I.

exchange of fire, were greater than the whole American strength in the engagement.

The episode at Carrizal resulted in a diplomatic crisis. A vociferous American minority demanded full-scale intervention in Mexico, but Wilson was too concerned with the progress of World War I in Europe, and with the possible involvement of the United States, to consider such a move. Even so, the president heeded the advice of the army chief of staff, Major General Hugh L. Scott, to use the facility granted to him just two weeks earlier by Congress to call the National Guard into federal service. This gave the army an additional 75,000 soldiers for the immensely difficult task of patrolling the Mexican border.

Wilson also persuaded Carranza to consider a diplomatic solution to the problem, and it was decided late in July 1916 to refer the disputes arising in general from the Punitive Expedition's actions, and in particular the Carrizal affair, to a joint commission for settlement. The commission later ruled that the Carrizal affair resulted from a fault by the American commander. The commission was dissolved in January 1917 before reaching agreeable solutions to other matters.

President Wilson now saw war with Germany as inevitable, and he therefore ordered the Punitive Expedition to return to the United States. The last elements of Pershing's force crossed the

A shore party of American sailors mans a machine gun during the Mexican War.

Mexican border on February 5, 1917. Even so, considerable tension remained between the United States and Mexico. This meant that during 1917 and 1918, a considerable body of American troops had to be kept on the border, where a small-scale guerrilla war continued.

In August 1918, this sporadic fighting flared up into a full battle. The scene was the twin towns of Nogales, neighbors on the frontier between Arizona and Sonora. A small incident soon escalated into heavy fighting that left American troops in control of the Mexican town by nightfall, but the U.S. force withdrew almost immediately in this last border skirmish before the United States became a dominant military force on the world stage.

Left: American sailors in action against Mexican snipers during May 1914.

Below: American soldiers show off a pile of captured Mexican weapons.

Glossary

Battalion: A basic subdivision of the regiment, generally less than 1,000 men and commanded by a lieutenant colonel.

Battery: The artillery counterpart to the infantry company.

Battleship: A major type of ship of the period, with heavy armament and heavy protection.

Blockade: A naval campaign to cut off access by closing the enemy's ports and coast.

Blockade runner: A ship used to break the enemy's blockade.

Blockhouse: A small fort providing its garrison with basic accommodation, protection, and firing positions.

Brigade: A basic unit of the division, including two or more regiments and commanded by a brigadier general.

Collier: A vessel designed to carry coal, an invaluable part of any naval force's movements in the days before oil-fired boilers.

Combined-arms operations: Operations undertaken jointly by two branches of a country's armed forces, generally the navy and army.

Company: The basic subdivision of the battalion, and generally commanded by a captain.

Corps: A primary component of the army, made up of two or more divisions and commanded in the U.S. Army by a major general but in most other armies by a lieutenant general.

Cruiser: A long-range warship between the destroyer and the battleship in size. It has two basic forms: a light or unarmored cruiser with 6-inch guns for raiding merchant shipping and a heavy or armored type with guns of 8-inch or greater caliber for fleet operations.

Destroyer: A comparatively small warship developed from the torpedo boat. It has torpedoes and guns of about 5-inch caliber and is used for independent or fleet operations. The destroyer relies on speed and agility to avoid enemy fire, not on armor to withstand such fire.

Division: The smallest army formation, including two or more brigades commanded by a major general. It is the basic army organization used for independent operations and therefore contains support elements (artillery, engineers, etc.) in addition to its infantry.

Dreadnought battleship: Named after the first such ship, the British H.M.S. *Dreadnought* which was completed in 1906, this was the ultimate battleship, its substantial main battery featured guns of a single caliber generally mounted on the ship's centerline. The first American dreadnoughts were the U.S.S. *South Carolina* and U.S.S. *Michigan* of the "South Carolina" class. They had a main battery of eight 12-inch guns in four twin turrets and a secondary battery of twenty-two 3-inch guns.

Entrenchments: Defensive positions created by digging a system of trenches and using the dirt to make raised parapets.

Flank: The extreme right or left side of a body of troops in a military position.

Formation: Any large body of troops with a capability to operate independently from the rest of the army. It therefore possesses (in addition to its organic infantry units) a full range of artillery, engineer, and support services. The smallest formation is generally the division.

Gatling gun: A primitive machine gun, generally of considerable size and weight, with a hand-cranked mechanism to rotate and operate the multi-barrel firing system.

Jingo: A blustering, unthinking person who favors aggressive patriotism.

Logistics: The science of planning and carrying out the movement of forces and their supplies.

Mine: An explosive device moored to a weight on the seabed and designed to float at the right depth under the surface of the water to explode when hit by the hull of an enemy ship.

Monitor: A warship of moderate size and low speed armed with a small number of heavy weapons and designed mainly for coastal operations against fortifications.

Munitions: Overall term for weapons and ammunition.

Pre-dreadnought battleship: A battleship of the period before the dreadnought battleship came into service in 1906. Such ships were comparatively slow, but were moderately well armored and had a mixed main gun armament. The last two American pre-dreadnoughts were the U.S.S. *Mississippi* and U.S.S. *Idaho* of the ''Mississippi'' class. They had a main battery of four 12-inch guns in two twin turrets, eight 8-inch guns in four twin turrets, and eight 7-inch guns in single mountings, as well as a secondary battery of twelve 3-inch guns.

Rearguard: The part of a unit of moving troops positioned at the very back, designed to protect the unit from attack from the rear.

Regiment: A basic tactical unit subordinate to the brigade. It is made up of two or more battalions and generally commanded by a colonel.

Sloop: A small warship with light armament but considerable endurance, intended mainly for operation on foreign stations.

Strategy: The art of winning a campaign or war by major operations.

Tactics: The art of winning a battle by minor operations.

Torpedo: A self-propelled underwater weapon able to keep its course and depth. It carries a large warhead which explodes on contact with the hull on an enemy vessel.

Torpedo boat: A light, high-speed vessel armed mainly with torpedoes and intended for attacks on the enemy's heavy warships.

Unit: Any small body of troops which is not capable of operations independent of the rest of the army. It therefore does not possess the full range of artillery, engineer, and support services. The largest unit is the brigade.

Bibliography

Conroy, Robert. *The Battle of Manila Bay: The Spanish American War in the Philippines.* (Macmillan, New York, 1968). For younger readers.

Downey, Fairfax. *Indian-Fighting Army.* (Charles Scribner's Sons, New York, 1941). Includes description of the army that went on to fight the Spanish-American War.

Dupuy, Col. R. Ernest and Major General William H. Baumer. *The Little Wars of the U.S.* (Hawthorn Books, New York, 1968).

Fleming, Peter. *The Siege at Peking.* (Harper & Brothers, New York, 1959). The Boxer Rebellion.

Friedel, Frank. *The Splendid Little War.* (Boston, 1958). The Spanish-American War.

Goldhurst, Richard. *Pipe Clay and Drill.* (Thomas Y. Crowell Co., New York, 1977). Biography of Pershing, including action in Mexico against Pancho Villa.

Hagan, Kenneth J. *American Gunboat Diplomacy and the Old Navy.* (Greenwood, Westport, CT, 1973).

Jones, Virgil Carrington. *Roosevelt's Rough Riders.* (Doubleday & Co., Garden City, NY, 1971).

Knox, Dudley W. *A History of the United States Navy.* (G. P. Putnam's Sons, New York, 1936).

Matthews, William and Dixon Wecter. *Our Soldiers Speak 1775-1918.* (Little Brown & Co., Boston, 1943).

O'Toole, G. J. A. *The Spanish War.* (W. W. Norton, New York, 1984).

Roosevelt, Theodore. *The Rough Riders.* (Charles Scribner's Sons, New York, 1903). Experiences in the Spanish-American War.

Thompson, H. C. *China and the Powers.* (Longmans Green & Co., London, 1902). The Boxer Rebellion.

Williams, T. Harry. *The History of American Wars from 1745 to 1918.* (Alfred A. Knopf, New York, 1981).

Young, James Rankin. *Reminisces and Thrilling Stories of the War by Returned Heroes.* (Wabash Publishing House, Chicago, 1898). First-person accounts of the Spanish-American War.

Index

Page numbers in *Italics* refer
to illustration